Introduction

Welcome

Ever since the commencement of the privatised railway network back in 1996, there have been times when passenger operators have needed to rely on loco-hauled trains in order to have sufficient rolling stock to operate their services. Frequently running on just a short or medium term basis, such resources were often hired in from one or more companies and could either take the form of just locomotives or coaching stock as well.

Over the past 25 years, such occurrences have brought loco-hauled trains to some unlikely lines with the formations typically being both short in length and normally top and tailed. The reasons for hiring in loco-hauled sets have varied widely but typically included a shortage of multiple units due to accident damage or maintenance issues, fluctuations in demand or just insufficient stock to run the advertised services.

In some instances, such hire-ins could last for quite extended periods, two particular examples of this being the fondly remembered Rhymney workings in South Wales along with operations along the North Wales coast to Holyhead while, more recently, enthusiasts have enjoyed last hurrahs in East Anglia and along the Cumbrian coast. However, the start ion ions e slam door coaches that formed , meaning that almost all regular loco-hauled passenger trains are now confined to those employing power door stock.

This publication looks back at this colourful and diverse era of hire-ins, considering locos paired with the passenger operators' own stock along with the deployment of trains formed of both hired motive power and coaches. I hope you find it of interest.

Simon Bendall - Editor

One of the few loco-hauled operations remaining is to be found on the Chiltern Railways London-Birmingham route, these services employing DRS-owned Class 68s and modernised Mk3 coaches. On July 5, 2018, 68012 has just left Marylebone as it powers through the urban canyon and towards Lords Tunnel with the 1N50 1721 departure to Bicester. (Simon McComb)

The sun has pretty much set on the operation of regular loco-hauled passenger trains with traditional slam doors following the introduction of new accessibility legislation at the beginning of 2020. With the exception of the exempt Night Riviera sleeper and a possible future return for Chiltern's Banbury commuter set, the last services to be withdrawn at the end of May were the ScotRail-operated Fife Circle workings following the expiry of their extension. Powered by DRS Class 68s for the past five years, the demise of the trains has also brought about the end of using Mk2 coaches on regular passenger services. On September 29, 2015, 68006 *Daring* traverses the magnificence of the Forth Bridge with the 2K14 1815 Glenrothes with Thornton to Edinburgh Waverley. (Robert McCulloch)

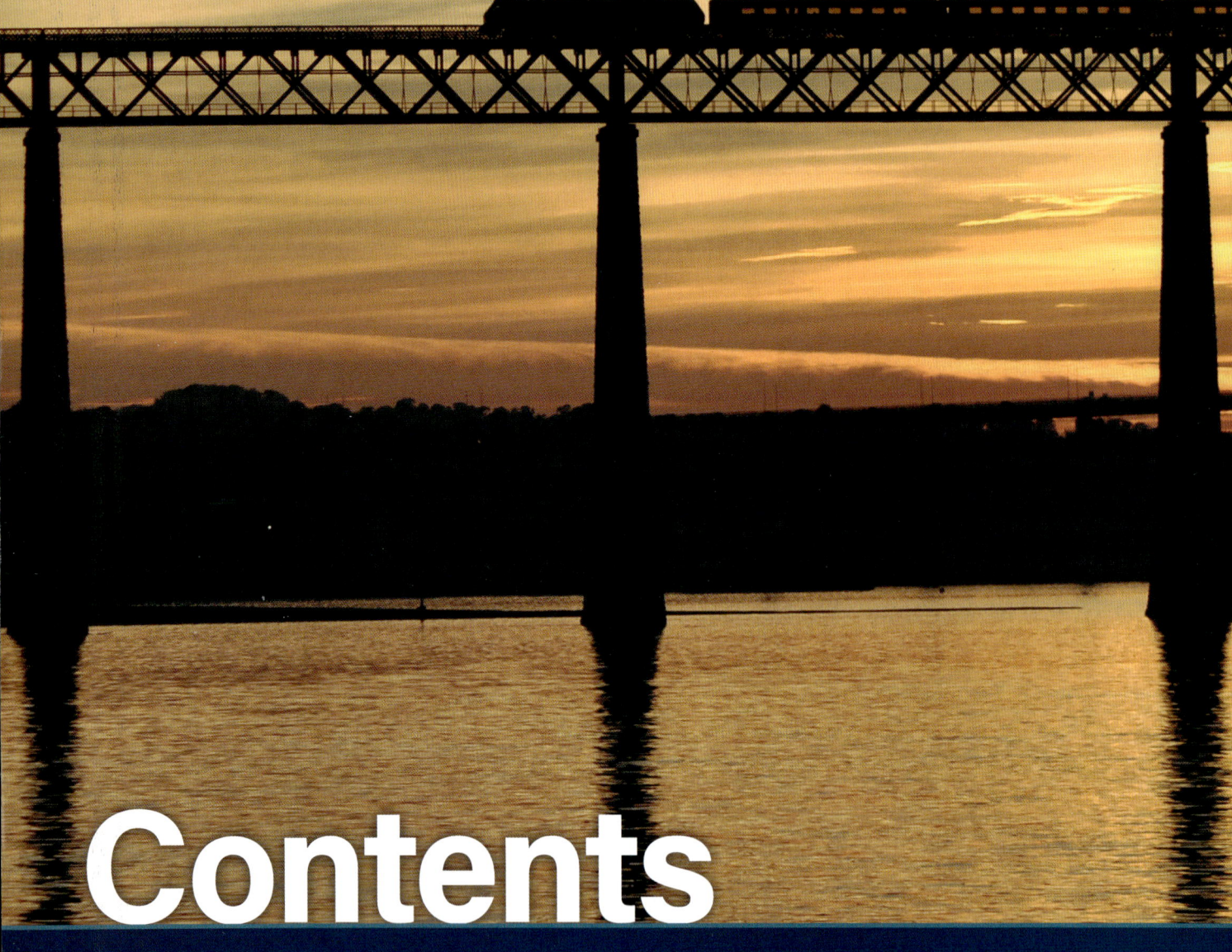

Contents

3	Welcome	48	Saturdays to Weekdays	
6	Weymouth and Beyond	56	Diesels in the Broads	
9	Backwater Trendsetters	66	Circling the Kingdom	
13	Thunder in the Valleys	71	Electrics Everywhere	
22	Along the Coast in Style	78	Through the Night	
29	Nationwide Assistance	90	Wrexham Wranglings	
36	Pedalling to the Seaside	96	The Call of the North	
40	Midland Miscellany	102	Wagging through Wales	
43	Shoving to Berwick	109	Rebirth for the Pennines	
44	Tractors Over the Top	112	A return to Rhymney	
46	East Coast Substitutes	114	Flying from the Fylde	

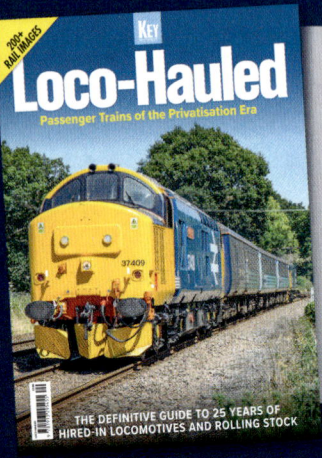

COVER IMAGE: Looking superb in BR large logo blue, 37409 *Lord Hinton* opens up through Brundall Gardens as it heads the 2C61 1355 Great Yarmouth-Norwich service for Greater Anglia on June 30, 2018, with 37407 on the rear. (Toby Radziszewski)

4 LOCO-HAULED - Passenger Trains of the Privatisation Era

Editor: Simon Bendall
Senior editor bookazines: Roger Mortimer
Email: roger.mortimer@keypublishing.com
Design: Dan Jarman
Cover design: Lee Howson

Advertising Sales Manager: Brodie Baxter
Email: brodie.baxter@keypublishing.com

Advertising Production: Rebecca Antoniades
Email: rebecca.antoniades@keypublishing.com

Subscriptions/Mail Order
Key Publishing Ltd, PO Box 300, Stamford, Lincs, PE9 1NA
Tel: 01780 480404 **Fax:** 01780 757812
Subscriptions email: subs@keypublishing.com
Mail Order email: orders@keypublishing.com
Website: www.keypublishing.com/shop

Publishing
Group CEO: Adrian Cox
Publisher: Mark Elliott
Chief Publishing Officer: Jonathan Jackson
Head of Production: Janet Watkins

Key Publishing Ltd, PO Box 100, Stamford, Lincs, PE9 1XP
Tel: 01780 755131
Website: www.keypublishing.com

Printing
Precision Colour Printing Ltd, Haldane, Halesfield 1, Telford, Shropshire. TF7 4QQ

Distribution
Seymour Distribution Ltd, 2 Poultry Avenue, London, EC1A 9PU
Enquiries Line: 02074 294000.

We are unable to guarantee the bonafides of any of our advertisers. Readers are strongly recommended to take their own precautions before parting with any information or item of value, including, but not limited to money, manuscripts, photographs or personal information in response to any advertisements within this publication.

© Key Publishing Ltd 2020
All rights reserved. No part of this magazine may be reproduced or transmitted in any form by any means, electronic or mechanical, including photocopying, recording or by any information storage and retrieval system, without prior permission in writing from the copyright owner. Multiple copying of the contents of the magazine without prior written approval is not permitted.

LOCO-HAULED - Passenger Trains of the Privatisation Era

South Wales & West

Weymouth and Beyond

With British Rail's Regional Railways sector having revitalised loco-hauled operations in several areas of the UK during the first half of the 1990s, this trend continued from 1994 with the break-up of the network in readiness for sale. While loco-hauled trains were most evident in north and south Wales, as subsequent chapters will show, they could also be found as part of the South Wales & West shadow franchise.

Continuing from Regional Railways days, there was a Class 37-powered diagram on the Cardiff-Bristol Temple Meads-Weymouth route in 1996 with additional workings from Cardiff to Birmingham New Street and Manchester Piccadilly depending on the day. These were booked for haulage by a Transrail Class 37/4, although substitutions by a Class 37/0 were far from unknown, while coaches were provided by a then embryonic West Coast Railway Company.

On a fine day in February 1996, 37412 *Driver John Elliott* rolls into Bristol Temple Meads with the 2V70 0840 service from Weymouth, not long after the loco-hauled workings had commenced. At this stage, the passenger stock was West Coast Mk1 TSOs pending the arrival of the Mk2s while a Mk1 Full Brake was on hire from Rail Express Systems to provide a brake vehicle and guard's accommodation. (Simon Bendall Collection)

Illustrating the other South Wales & West loco-hauled route, sister Transrail machine 37411 is seen approaching Droitwich on June 16, 1996, with the Sundays-only 1V19 1900 Birmingham New Street-Cardiff Central. The train had just traversed the single line from Stoke Works Junction and is joining the main line from Kidderminster. Unsurprisingly, the weekend working was popular with haulage enthusiasts! (Martin Loader)

6 LOCO-HAULED - Passenger Trains of the Privatisation Era

South Wales & West

It was relatively common to find freight-only Class 37s on the Weymouth workings, especially during the warmer months when the lack of an electric train supply was not such a problem. For a handful of days in June 1996, celebrity 37116 *Sister Dora* was deployed and is seen setting out from Bristol Temple Meads with the 2O93 1633 working to Weymouth on June 24th. (Simon Bendall Collection)

Once part of the Motherwell fleet, 37427 *Highland Enterprise* was Cardiff-based when photographed at Croome on a fine August 4, 1996, with the 1M15 1610 Cardiff Central-Birmingham New Street. It would later return south with the 1V19 1900 Birmingham New Street-Cardiff. Of the eight Class 37/4s that received the Regional Railways colours, 37427 was unique in carrying ScotRail lettering. (Martin Loader)

With Wisconsin Central having arrived on the UK freight scene two years earlier, the EWS brand and livery were well established by the spring of 1998 as shown by 37411, which was now named *Ty Hafan*. Pictured at Defford, to the south of Worcester, on May 17, the English Electric machine was in charge of the 1M15 1610 Cardiff Central-Birmingham New Street. This was the final day of this working, it and the corresponding 1V19 1940 return reverting to a DMU with the implementation of the summer timetable. (Martin Loader)

A fleet of eight Mk2b and Mk2c coaches was made available, of which Tourist Standard Open (TSO) 5463, 5487 and 5569 along with Brake Standard Open (BSO) 9448 carried BR maroon. In contrast, TSOs 5453/78/91 and BSO 9440 were given a smart dark blue South Wales & West livery. In addition, three maroon-liveried Mk1 TSOs, 99318/27/28, were initially provided in the spring of 1996 while some of the Mk2s were being prepared for service. Normally running in four-coach sets, these could be lengthened as required with five, six and seven coaches being noted on occasions. Additionally, with the two liveries evenly split, mixed rakes of both was a standard occurrence.

These trains continued to operate during 1997 and 1998 to a largely unchanged route and formation, although with the acquisition of Transrail by EWS in 1996, maroon and gold liveried Class 37/4s were frequently found up front. Meanwhile, October 1996 had seen Prism Rail win the franchise, becoming Wales & West. Inevitably, a re-deployment of Diesel Multiple Units (DMUs) at the end of 1999 saw the loco-hauled workings come to an end that September.

LOCO-HAULED - Passenger Trains of the Privatisation Era 7

South Wales & West

Despite appearances, 37431 was just 11 months from withdrawal as it heads the Sundays-only 1625 Weymouth to Bristol Temple Meads on the single line from Blatchbridge Junction into Frome. Pictured on May 31, 1998, the Mainline-liveried Type 3 would be withdrawn in April 1999 as EWS culled its older traction as the Class 66s arrived, it quickly being disposed of at Wigan in January 2000. (Mark Few)

The use of Class 47s on the Weymouth diagram was by no means unknown, the presence of the Rail Express Systems depot at Bristol Barton Hill meaning an example was usually available when needed. Such was the case on April 27, 1999, as 47584 stands at its destination of Westbury after arriving with the 2V93 1938 from Weymouth. This was one of a handful of RES Class 47s to avoid the life extension modifications in the early 1990s and consequently was not renumbered into the '47/7' series. The loco's *The Locomotive and Carriage Institution* nameplates were also highly unusual in featuring a circular design. (Mark Few)

With just four months to go before the loco-hauled workings ceased, 37409 *Loch Awe* has just departed Frome as it passes the former Butler & Tanner print works at the head of the 2O87 0900 Bristol Temple Meads-Weymouth on May 22, 1999. At this time, the Scottish favourite was still based at Motherwell but enjoying a holiday in the south, the depot's Class 37/4s sometimes being called upon to assist if the availability of the Cardiff examples was low. (Mark Few)

8 LOCO-HAULED - Passenger Trains of the Privatisation Era

Silverlink

Backwater Trendsetters

October 1998 brought the first instance of a top and tailed loco-hauled formation substituting for a multiple unit. And it happened on an unlikely route when Silverlink deployed a pair of Fragonset Class 31s to work with just two Forward Trust Mk2 coaches over the Marston Vale line between Bedford and Bletchley. Hired in for a week to cover for a maintenance backlog on the operator's increasingly decrepit Class 117 and Class 121 DMU fleets, it was a novel if expensive way of maintaining a service. By having a loco at either end of the train, this eliminated the need to run-round, even if the track and signalling layout would permit it, while the arrangement also allowed quicker reversals, enabling a timetable designed for multiple unit operation to be more or less maintained. Having only just returned to service under the ownership of the then fledging hire company, 31452 and 31468 were the locos deployed on the workings.

The Brush Type 2s returned for a much longer stint during the following year. Commencing at the end of March 1999 and running throughout the summer, two pairs of Class 31s were provided by Fragonset this time around, albeit with the second loco-hauled set starting somewhat later than the first. In addition to 31452 and 31468, other resurrected locos also appeared in the form of 31459 along with newly modified 31601 and 31602, this latter pair having been modified with through wiring for an electric train supply. This time around, it was Riviera Trains that provided the coaching stock.

Illustrating the first week-long dalliance with Class 31 power on the Marston Vale line, 31452 is seen approaching Millbrook with the 1146 Bedford to Bletchley service on October 12, 1998, with 31468 on the rear. With plenty of power available for the two-coach train, this was made up of Mk2a coaches from the Forward Trust fleet in the form of Tourist Standard Open (TSO) 5376 and Brake Standard Open (BSO) 9417. (Martin Loader)

LOCO-HAULED - Passenger Trains of the Privatisation Era 9

Silverlink

August 1999 also saw Silverlink bring loco-haulage, albeit for just a few days, to the Gospel Oak-Barking line in London as availability of its first generation DMUs plummeted yet further. This saw Cambrian Trains' push-pull 'Crompton' 33103 paired with former Network South East Class 438 charter unit 417, this still carrying its BR blue livery applied in the early 1990s. However, by this time, the first of Silverlink's replacement Class 150/1 'Sprinters' had begun to arrive from Central Trains, having been displaced from the West Midlands by the new Class 170 'Turbostars'. This development brought the demise of both loco-hauled operations along with the heritage DMUs they were covering for.

It was not until September 2004 that Silverlink was forced to return to loco-haulage and then in a very different form as it introduced peak-hour workings between London Euston and Northampton to bolster capacity as part of a timetable recast. These were normally powered by Class 90s hired from EWS, although the few Class 87s remaining with Virgin Trains at this time also put in appearances. Two Mk.3 rakes were specially formed up consisting of a Driving Van Trailer (DVT), one First Open (FO) and eight Tourist Standard Opens (TSO), all in de-branded Virgin colours.

Based at Wembley, the 'Cobbler' sets shared resources with the handful of Virgin West Coast Mk3 rakes that remained following the introduction of the 'Pendolinos'. This meant that DVTs in the modified Virgin red livery with black window surrounds/cab doors and an enlarged yellow warning panel saw use on the Northampton services alongside those retaining the original incarnation of the red and grey scheme. The Silverlink workings ceased in July 2005 as the Class 350/1 'Desiros' entered service.

When the Class 31s returned to the Bedford-Bletchley route from March 1999, initially only one diagram was worked by the Fragonset machines with a DMU remaining on the other. The coaches were also different with a pair of Riviera Trains Mk1s provided in the shape of TSO 5025 and Brake Standard Corridor (BSK) 35452, both in chocolate and cream. On April 1, 31452 tails the 1250 to Bedford as 31468 powers away from Woburn Sands. *(Phil Chilton)*

By May 27, 1999, the coaching stock had swapped over to Mk2d air conditioned vehicles, again from the Riviera Trains fleet. In this instance, the 0940 Bedford-Bletchley was made up of TSO 5630 and Brake First Corridor (BFK) 17164, both still carrying their defunct Waterman Railways colours but with Riviera lettering. For passengers long used to the rattily open interiors of DMUs, the compartments of the brake coach must have been a novel change! With 31601 *Bletchley Park 'Station X'* up front, 31468 was the tail-gunner as the formation departs Kempton Hardwick station. *(Martin Loader)*

Silverlink

The other set of Riviera Mk2d coaches were recorded forming the 1050 Bletchley-Bedford on July 24, 1999, as 31459 *Cerberus* approaches Berry Lane level crossing, Aspley Guise, with 31602 *Chimaera* at the back. This was a mixed livery set with BFK 17159 carrying chocolate and cream while 5630 was again in the LNWR-derived Waterman Railways livery. (Bill Atkinson)

Falling squarely in the outrageous category was the use of 33103 on the Gospel Oak to Barking route for less than a week in August 1999. This saw it partnered with an unpowered TC unit to allow push-pull operation, the EMU running in three-car formation with its Trailer First Corridor car removed. So short-lived were the workings that many enthusiasts never got to see or sample a 'Crompton' bombing around North and East London on scheduled passenger trains, with 33103 seen pushing the TC away from South Tottenham. (Stuart Pearce)

The return of peak-hour loco-hauled trains to the Euston-Northampton route in 2004 for the first time since 1990 was as welcome as it was unexpected, the limited-stop Silverlink services providing some much needed additional capacity for commuters. A colourful array of AC electrics was utilised over the 10 month operation, including EWS-owned 90024, which is seen passing Carpenders Park on May 25, 2005, with the 1W99 1821 Euston-Northampton. Carrying GNER livery, this was a legacy of an earlier period when EWS hired a Class 90 to the operator to supplement its Class 91 fleet, although 90024 became somewhat infamous for being found anywhere but on the East Coast Main Line! (Jonathan Lewis)

LOCO-HAULED - Passenger Trains of the Privatisation Era **11**

Silverlink

As well as EWS Class 90s, the Silverlink services sometimes featured Class 87s, these coming from a pool retained at Willesden to work the few loco-hauled diagrams that remained with Virgin Trains after the mass introduction of the 'Pendolinos'. During February 2005, 87012 was repainted into Network South East colours, the livery serving as a patriotic background for slogans promoting the bid for London to host the 2012 Olympics. Four months later, on July 8 and named *The Olympian,* 87012 is seen on the down slow outside Leighton Buzzard and slowing for the station stop while again powering the 1W99 'Cobbler' to Northampton. (David Smith)

With just over a month to go before the end, an early start was required to catch 90023 arriving at Northampton with the 5W96 0522 empty stock working from Wembley on June 8, 2005. This would return to London as the 1W96 0733 to Euston, there being two southbound workings on weekday mornings and corresponding returns in the early evening. (David Smith)

12 LOCO-HAULED - Passenger Trains of the Privatisation Era

South Wales

Thunder in the Valleys

Highlighting some of the entrepreneurial spirit that existed in the earliest days of privatisation, 1995 saw a loco-hauled service introduced on the Rhymney line during peak hours. This created extra capacity on the busy commuter services to Cardiff and also allowed the DMUs released to be used to strengthen services elsewhere. Organised by the Cardiff Valleys train operating unit, the workings were initially supported by Waterman Railways, which supplied its Class 47s, with a selection of Mk2 coaches coming from the associated Carriage & Traction Company. Rail Express Systems Type 4s also featured heavily going forward into 1996, working alongside their Waterman classmates, while October of that year saw Prism Rail, trading as the Cardiff Railway Company (CRC), awarded the franchise with the hauled set being retained.

Following the break-up of Waterman Railways, EWS Class 37/4s began their long and celebrated association with the Rhymney workings from June 1997. The next major development came from the start of January 1998 with the arrival of the 71A Group's BR green Class 33 D6593 (33208) for use on the Rhymneys, this covering one diagram with an EWS '37/4' on the other. Unfortunately, a serious failure put the 'Crompton' out of action after only five months with CRC instead turning to the Fifty Fund to hire 50031 for the summer season.

The autumn of 1999 was an important one for the railways in South Wales as the Rugby World Cup arrived, bringing a huge increase in passenger numbers. With extra loco-hauled trains drafted in, this brought Fragonset Class 31s to the valleys on Bargoed shuttles and, when they played up, Freightliner and EWS Class 47s as well, these working alongside the already present '37s' and '50s'.

Moving into the 2000s and with the excitement of the rugby over, the EWS Class 37s more or less achieved dominance on the Rhymney workings for their remaining years, an assortment of colourful '37/4s' plying back and forth with the odd bit of assistance from Class 47s on occasions. Meanwhile, July 2002 saw the reorganised and renamed Wales & Borders franchise introduce a daily loco-hauled working to Fishguard Harbour utilising stock from the Rhymney services and a Class 37/4, workings which were repeated during 2003.

From December 2003, Arriva Trains Wales took over the Welsh franchise, it continuing with the Fishguard trains the next year. Although the Rhymney workings were planned to come to an end in December 2005, they lingered on for another 12 months but reduced to just one diagram. Arriva was also not quite finished with loco-haulage elsewhere as December 2005 brought ad-hoc workings to Gloucester and Fishguard, using EWS Class 37/4s and the company's own blue-painted Mk2e/f stock, as DMU availability dropped.

The summer of 2006 brought regular Class 50 operation to Fishguard as 50031 and 50049 were hired for a daily service between June and September, powering Arriva Mk2s. The duo also saw use on various reliefs and specials in connection with events at the Millennium Stadium during the year. Arriva's final dalliance with loco-hauled services took place in March 2007 with Riviera Class 47s deployed on rugby specials, this bringing to a close 12 years of interesting and creative operations.

The first two years of the Rhymney workings employed Waterman Class 47s supported by Rail Express Systems classmates. With the set not required at weekends, it was free to be used elsewhere in South Wales, such as providing additional capacity when major sporting events were being held at Cardiff. On June 2, 1996, 47712 Dick Whittington arrives at Taffs Well with the 2A10 1300 Merthyr Tydfil to Barry Island, this being loco-hauled in connection with the Road Transport Festival at the latter location. Just visible on the rear for top and tail operation is 37254. (Martin Loader)

LOCO-HAULED - Passenger Trains of the Privatisation Era 13

South Wales

The EWS Class 37/4s came to the Rhymney Valley from the early summer of 1997, replacing the Class 47s. A year later, on May 1, 1998, the late afternoon 2O43 1704 Cardiff Central to Rhymney commuter service was in the hands of 37411 *Ty Hafan* as it passes Pontlottyn. Six Carriage & Traction Company Mk2d coaches were available for the set, TSOs 5630, 5647, 5732 and 5739 along with BFKs 17141 and 17164, all carrying the LNWR-derived Waterman Railways livery. Four were typically used with the other two as maintenance spares.
(Martin Loader)

Unfortunately, 33208 only lasted five months in South Wales at the beginning of 1998, a generator failure curtailing its time on the Rhymney services. Although repairs were completed by the autumn, its time had passed and it was no longer required by the Cardiff Railway Company. However, with the Rugby World Cup taking place in Wales during October 1999, the 'Crompton' made a return to South Wales two months beforehand as Wales & West prepared for the additional loco-hauled services that would be needed to cope with the increased passenger numbers. On August 17, 33208 is seen at Newport working a 1020 Crewe to Cardiff driver familiarisation run that also acted as a relief service.
(Jim Ramsay)

After 33208's expiry, Cardiff Railway Company brought in a replacement in the form of 50031 *Hood*, this working the Rhymneys between June and September before returning again in 1999 with newly completed 50044 for company. In addition, it was deployed on other weekend specials around South Wales, including visiting Treherbert and Merthyr Tydfil. On July 21, 1998, English Electric music reverberates across Pontlottyn as the 'Hoover' accelerates away with the 2R05 1705 Cardiff-Rhymney.
(Martin Loader)

14 LOCO-HAULED - Passenger Trains of the Privatisation Era

South Wales

In the run up to the actual Rugby World Cup, a number of warm up matches were held at the Millennium Stadium in Cardiff, these being used to test the enhanced train service. With additional locos required, freight-only Class 37s were drafted in as demonstrated by 37371 as it arrives at Bargoed with the 2F37 1415 Rhymney-Cardiff on August 21, 1999. In tow is a set of Forward Trust (later HSBC) Mk2a coaches, the first rake of these having arrived in the valleys in January 1998 following refurbishment.
(Phil Chilton)

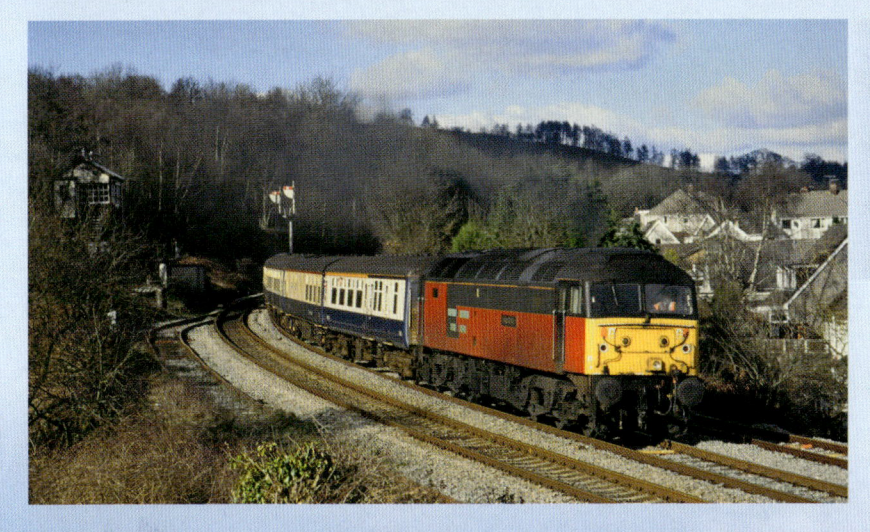

Further rugby matches in February 2000 brought the running of Bargoed to Cardiff shuttles on two Saturdays during the month. On the second occasion, the 19th, 47721 *Saint Bede* is seen passing the 'box at Ystrad Mynach with the 2D12 1416 departure to Cardiff. Bringing up the rear but out of sight was 47306 *The Sapper* while a second set that day featured 47775 *Respite* and 47798 *Prince William*.
(Jason Cross)

Relieved of its prestigious Royal Scotsman duties, maroon-liveried but now de-named 37428 had swapped the Scottish Highlands for South Wales by May 18, 2001. Seen departing Bargoed, the Type 3 was in charge of the 2V07 0723 Rhymney-Radyr. By this time, the former Forward Trust Mk2a coaches had departed following their sale to Riviera Trains by HSBC and been replaced on a short term basis by Regional Railways-liveried Mk2a stock transferred from the North Wales coast. (Mark Few)

LOCO-HAULED - Passenger Trains of the Privatisation Era

South Wales

By August 31, 2002, the coaching stock had been altered once more with West Coast-owned Mk2b/c making up the 2F34 1415 Rhymney-Cardiff. These had arrived 14 months earlier, having been fitted with central door locking equipment beforehand. With a fresh coat of EWS maroon recently applied, in charge at Pontlottyn was 37408 *Loch Rannoch*, the hugely popular 'Tractor' being three years away from its career-ending collision at Rhymney. (Phil Chilton)

Previously in tatty and unbranded Railfreight triple grey, 37402 *Bont Y Bermo* was another English Electric machine with a fresh coat of paint at Tirphil on June 7, 2003. With different shades of grey employed, either deliberately or not, the result was certainly a unique variation on the livery. On this day, it was atop the 1B96 0911 Rhymney to Fishguard Harbour, the extended workings into West Wales certainly bringing welcome additional mileage. At this time, the stock remained the West Coast pressure-ventilated Mk2s, now with added Valley Lines logos, while air-conditioned Mk2d/e from the same company had also arrived in South Wales the previous year. However, from the following month, Riviera Trains took over as the rolling stock provider, deploying de-branded Virgin Trains Mk.2e/f coaches instead. (Martin Loader)

16 LOCO-HAULED - Passenger Trains of the Privatisation Era

South Wales

On the evening of August 1, 2005, 37408 ran away during shunting operations at Rhymney, it suffering a dropped nose in the subsequent collision with a rake of Mk2 coaches while 37425 on the other end also sustained damage as the coaches were propelled forward. With 37411 additionally stopped for repairs, emergency replacements to resolve the traction shortage came from Riviera Trains in the form of 47839, 47847 and 47848, these working on the Rhymneys for five weeks. On August 27, 47847 *Brian Morrison/Railway World Magazine* heads the 2F38 1515 Rhymney-Cardiff at Ystrad Mynach. (Jason Cross)

With 2005 scheduled to be the last year of the Rhymney services, Arriva Trains Wales arranged for 37425 to be repainted by EWS into BR large logo blue that April to see out the rest of the year, although the subsequent 12 month extension of one diagram gave an extended goodbye. On July 9, 2005, 37425 rumbles into Ystrad Mynach with the 2F26 1215 Rhymney-Cardiff. Leading the formation are some of the ex Virgin Mk2 'air-cons' hired from Riviera Trains.
(Simon Bendall Collection)

A second Class 37/4 was repainted for the Rhymney swansong in the form of 37411, this being returned to more or less its original livery and named *Caerphilly Castle*. In sparkling condition fresh from the Toton paintshop but yet to gain its nameplates, the green machine slogs away from Bargoed with the 2R10 0859 Cardiff-Rhymney on May 21, 2005. (Mark Few)

LOCO-HAULED - Passenger Trains of the Privatisation Era 17

South Wales

During 2006, only one Rhymney diagram remained in operation following the arrival of additional DMUs at Cardiff Canton. Still, one was better than none and the use of Arriva's own attractively-painted Mk2 stock created some new colour combinations. With its *Pride of the Valleys/Balchder y Cymoedd* nameplates now applied and some weathering acquired, 37425 looks even better in large logo blue as it thrashes away from Rhymney atop the 2F10 0744 working to Cardiff on August 12. (Phil Chilton)

On a day of rugby-related specials, the early morning fog had just about burned away at Purton as the 2Z37 0815 Gloucester-Cardiff skirts the Severn estuary on November 4, 2006. Leading the way was 37410 *Aluminium 100* with 37406 *The Saltire Society* on the rear; at this time 37410 was carrying unofficial replacement name stickers after one if its nameplates was stolen in March 2003 and the other subsequently removed. (Phil Chilton)

18 LOCO-HAULED - Passenger Trains of the Privatisation Era

South Wales

Where there were once Class 33s, non-heat Class 37s and others, the Crewe-Cardiff rugby specials on November 4, 2006, featured rather less interesting traction in the form of Class 67s, although seeing the Spanish-built GMs on the Arriva stock was still novel. Powering the 1V75 0918 Crewe-Cardiff on this day was 67023 as it passed Long Dyke Junction, Splott, and neared its destination. Several variations in the application of the Arriva livery to the Mk2s were discernible if paying attention, for example the third and fourth TSOs in this set lacked the yellow stripe. (Phil Chilton)

The rugby specials of March 17, 2007, brought to a close the era of franchise-operated loco-hauled workings in South Wales. Somewhat appropriately, it was Sulzer-powered machinery that was in charge for the final day given Class 47s had launched the first services back in 1995. Hired in from Riviera Trains, 47812 leads the 2Z59 1358 Gloucester-Cardiff pass Purton once again with its equally green sister 47815 bringing up the rear. (Jonathan Lewis)

LOCO-HAULED - Passenger Trains of the Privatisation Era

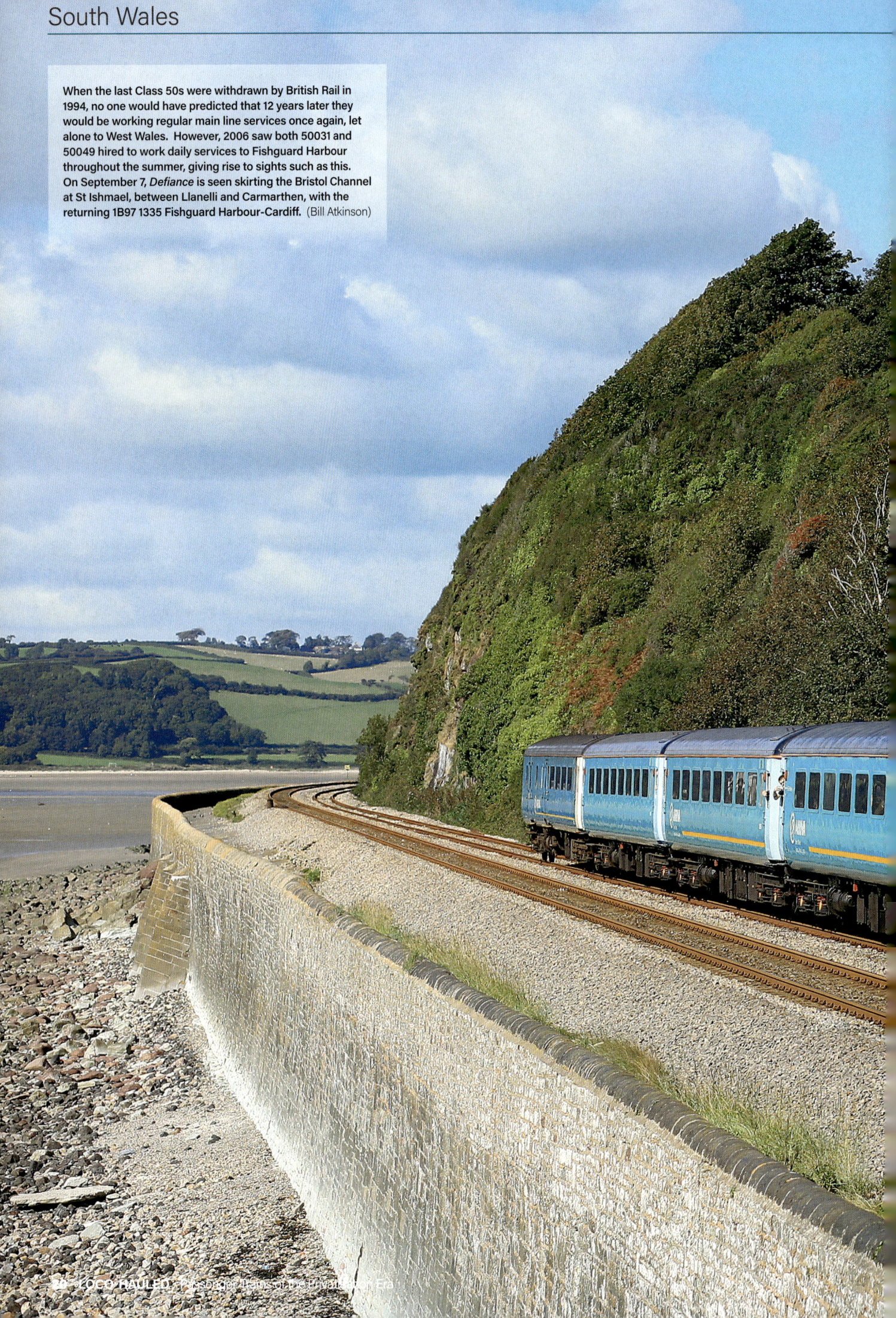

South Wales

When the last Class 50s were withdrawn by British Rail in 1994, no one would have predicted that 12 years later they would be working regular main line services once again, let alone to West Wales. However, 2006 saw both 50031 and 50049 hired to work daily services to Fishguard Harbour throughout the summer, giving rise to sights such as this. On September 7, *Defiance* is seen skirting the Bristol Channel at St Ishmael, between Llanelli and Carmarthen, with the returning 1B97 1335 Fishguard Harbour-Cardiff. (Bill Atkinson)

South Wales

North Wales

Along the Coast in Style

Much like the South Wales & West franchise, the Class 37-hauled trains along the North Wales coast were already established when the franchising process commenced, having been introduced by Regional Railways in 1993. When North Western Trains took over in March 1997, these hugely popular workings continued as before but an order for replacement Class 175 DMUs was formally placed just over a year later, around the same time as First Group took full control of the franchise after buying out its partners and later renaming it First North Western.

Deliveries of the Class 175s commenced in the autumn of 1999 but their introduction into service was a difficult and protracted affair due to technical issues. Consequently, the Class 37s gained several stays of execution as replacement dates came and went. Eventually though, the Alstom-built units were deemed reliable enough and available in sufficient numbers to officially take over from December 30, 2000. Even then, a small handful of Class 37 workings still took place in January 2001, with the very last one on January 20, 2000.

However, this was not the end of loco-haulage on the coast as numerous reliability issues with the Class 175s forced First North Western to reintroduce a hauled set from June 2002 but using an EWS Class 47 this time around with a diagram from Holyhead to Manchester, which was altered to a Bangor-Manchester working at the end of the year. With the DMUs requiring extensive modifications, more hauled sets were introduced as cover from March 2003, these continuing until March 2004 even after the North Wales coast and other routes had transferred to the control of Arriva Trains Wales during September 2003.

Even then, a further comeback occurred between September 2004 and February 2005, this time with Riviera Trains resources and running initially between Holyhead-Crewe and then Holyhead/Chester to Manchester Piccadilly. Next to step up for a go were Class 57/3s, a single diagram operating between Holyhead and Manchester from December 2005 to the summer of 2006 after Class 175s were temporarily lost for collision damage repairs.

Two months after North Western Trains, later to become First North Western, had commenced its tenure of the franchise, 37408 *Loch Rannoch* powers through Sandycroft with the 1H44 1323 Holyhead to Manchester Piccadilly 'Irish Mancunian' on May 31, 1997. The loco would lose its popular BR large logo livery the following year but, after a considerable backlash from enthusiasts, the nameplates were allowed to remain. (Martin Loader)

North Wales

Prior to the arrival of EWS, it was Transrail that supplied Class 37/4s for use along the coast. On May 24, 1997, 37423 *Sir Murray Morrison* was still displaying the now obsolete emblem as it passed Llanfairfechan with a morning departure from Holyhead. From the summer of 1996, a hire agreement with Riviera Trains had seen a number of Mk1 TSOs provided to allow strengthening of the sets, these all carrying BR chocolate/cream and thus rather stood out. (Tony Woof)

The use of freight-only Class 37s was a fairly regular occurrence at times, particularly during the warmer months. On July 15, 2000, 37710 was given a rare run out after the booked '37/4' expired the previous evening. Seen on the approach to Rhyl, the Loadhaul machine was in charge of the 1K57 0749 Holyhead-Crewe but was removed from the set immediately after reaching its destination. (Phil Chilton)

LOCO-HAULED - Passenger Trains of the Privatisation Era

North Wales

A large proportion of the Class 37/4 fleet put in an appearance on the coast during the eight years of loco-hauled services, including some of the Scottish-based examples. On June 24, 2000, Royal Scotsman liveried 37428 was doing its bit for the fleet as it passes Penmaenmawr with the 1D79 1719 Crewe-Holyhead. The loco was 'borrowed' whilst on its way south to Cardiff for wheelset work. (Phil Chilton)

In contrast to the coastal vistas available on the mainland, the Isle of Anglesey offered less dramatic backdrops but was still worth photographing nonetheless. On May 13, 2000, the gorse-dominated Tywyn Trewan Common nature reserve at Valley dominates the view as 37429 *Eisteddfod Genedlaethol* rumbles by with the 1D75 1423 Birmingham New Street to Holyhead. (Martin Loader)

24 LOCO-HAULED - Passenger Trains of the Privatisation Era

North Wales

Conwy Castle and the town's mediaeval walls have long served as an imposing backdrop for photos. Amongst the many interesting views is that of the arch created in 1847 to allow the Chester and Holyhead Railway to pass through the wall, it being designed to match its surroundings. On July 15, 2000, 37426 sweeps through while heading the 1G11 1403 Holyhead to Birmingham New Street. (Terry Eyres)

In the final summer of 'Tractors' along the coast, the doyen of the Class 37/4s, 37401 *Mary Queen of Scots*, powers along past Mochdre, between Llandudno Junction and Colwyn Bay, with the 1K57 0749 Holyhead-Crewe on August 19, 2000. As well as the Riviera Mk1 TSO, two other Regional Railways examples are included at the back of the train, these running to the very end alongside the pressure ventilated Mk2s. (Phil Chilton)

North Wales

When loco-hauled trains returned to the North Wales coast in June 2002, it was the turn of Class 47s to show what they could do. In the first month of operation on June 11, 47757 *Restitution* hurries the 1D67 1007 Birmingham International to Holyhead along near Penmaenmawr. The Mk2 coaches were on loan to First North Western from sister franchise First Great Western. (Neil Harvey)

Although EWS held the contract to supply the traction for the revitalised workings, the increase in diagrams during 2003 meant it sometimes struggled to provide enough Class 47s. With Riviera Trains being based in Crewe, it was easy enough to hire one of their Type 4s if the need arose. Such was the case on August 2, 2003, when 47839 was recorded passing through Slindon with the 1D82 1721 Birmingham New Street-Holyhead, its Oxford blue paintwork still being fresh after a repaint at the beginning of the year. (Terry Eyres)

North Wales

As well as Rail Express Systems-liveried Class 47s, EWS examples also appeared on the coast diagrams. Such was the case on May 14, 2003, as Royal train reserve loco 47787 *Windsor Castle* powered through Moore, Cheshire, and into the evening with the 1D45 1719 Manchester Piccadilly-Holyhead. Ten months later, the workings came to an end, which was something of a relief for EWS as it looked to eliminate the remainder of its Class 47 fleet. (John Eyres)

When loco-hauled cover for the Class 175s was required yet again from September 2004, it was Riviera Trains that was handed the task of providing both locos and coaches. On September 7, Fragonset's 47832 was deployed to handle the 1D37 1000 Manchester Piccadilly to Holyhead, this still retaining its First Great Western colours but with additional white Fragonset branding. Seen passing Penmaenmawr, the former Virgin Mk2s were from the Riviera stable. (John Eyres)

In its attractive XP64 blue livery, Riviera's 47853 *Rail Express* pauses at Rhyl on August 21, 2004, with the late-running 1K96 0854 Holyhead-Crewe, having lost some 45 minutes on this Saturday working at this point. This particular batch of hauled workings continued until February 2005. (Andy Williams)

LOCO-HAULED - Passenger Trains of the Privatisation Era

North Wales

Making more comebacks than an ageing rock band, it was the turn of the Class 57/3s to have fun along the coast when a hauled set was required to cover for damaged DMUs from December 2005. Future 'WAG' loco 57315 *The Mole* was already becoming accustomed to the scenery around Valley as it heads for the Britannia Bridge with the 1H90 1320 Holyhead-Manchester Piccadilly. The date is July 15, 2006, a month before the diagram ceased. (Jimmy Wilson)

The autumn of 2007 saw Arriva Trains Wales making plans for another period of Class 175 replacement workings using a Class 67 and its own Mk2 stock made redundant from the South Wales workings. In the event, a shuffle of units meant the set was not needed but the preparations progressed as far as carrying out driver training. On October 2, the soon to be Wrexham & Shropshire liveried 67014 passes Bagillt with the 5K67 1448 Holyhead-Crewe Carriage Sidings training run. Notably, the Mk2f BSO behind the loco is from the original Arriva Trains Northern set, the different shade of blue marking it out from the three TSOs.
(David Rapson)

28 LOCO-HAULED - Passenger Trains of the Privatisation Era

Virgin Trains

Nationwide Assistance

When it was created in the run up to privatisation, the Cross Country train operating unit was the largest in the country in terms of the area covered. This stretched from Penzance and Swansea along with Poole, Portsmouth and Brighton through the West Midlands to the Northwest, Northeast and onwards to Edinburgh and Aberdeen. With the franchise awarded to Virgin Trains, operations commenced from January 5, 1997, utilising a mixed fleet of HSTs, Class 47 and Class 86 loco-hauled sets and a mere five Class 158s.

With a loco fleet aged between 30 and 35 years racking up hundreds of miles every day, it was no great surprise that reliability was patchy and, at times, worse than this. Within a year, Cross Country was seeking to hire in additional locos to help out as required, this including Class 47s from Fragonset and EWS with the latter also providing Class 86s for use on the northern section of the West Coast Main Line. Most outlandish of all was the hiring of 'Deltic' D9000 to work a summer Saturday service to Ramsgate during both 1998 and 1999.

Deals were struck with EWS for the long term hire of Class 47s, these mostly receiving Virgin colours as part of the arrangement, while the late 1990s and early 2000s saw frequent use of all manner of freight locos, some of these workings becoming legendary for the rarity of motive power or the destination reached. Virgin's sister West Coast franchise also had the need to call on assisting locos, be it for failures, diversionary drags or the direct services over the un-electrified North Wales coast to Holyhead.

Naturally, such chaos could not last with the new Bombardier-built 'Voyagers' entering traffic from May 2001, it taking until August 2002 to dispense with the last loco-hauled Cross Country workings. Whether the Class 220s and Class 221s were an improvement for the franchise is debatable, given the subsequent culling of services that was made in 2003 after the capacity of the units proved to be woefully inadequate.

The small fleet of Class 47s operated by Fragonset were near permanent fixtures on Virgin Cross Country services in the late 1990s. Of these, 47712 was a particularly solid performer, it retaining de-branded Waterman Railways black long after its stablemates had been repainted. On May 18, 1998, the well-travelled Type 4 is seen powering away from the outskirts of Oxford at Wolvercote Junction, having just passed under the A34. Bound for Liverpool Lime Street, it was working the 1M79 1647 departure from Reading. (Martin Loader)

Virgin Trains

Among the services inherited by Virgin Cross Country were those between Manchester Airport and Edinburgh Waverley, which brought with it an allocation of five Class 158s, 158747-51. However, on September 10, 1999, a substitute loco-hauled set had been turned out for the 1S45 0556 Manchester Airport-Edinburgh with BR two-tone green 47488 leading a shortened rake of Mk2s and 47705 *Guy Fawkes* in plain black. While both were previously part of the Waterman fleet, by this date 47488 belonged to Fragonset while 47705 was owned by Riviera Trains. Seen at Greenholme, the Type 4s would pass by again that evening with the 1M04 1857 departure back to Manchester. (David Dockray)

The hiring of D9000 to work to Ramsgate on summer Saturdays in both 1998 and 1999 was outlandish even by Virgin's standards but, with every train well-loaded with enthusiasts, it brought in plenty of extra revenue. On August 8, 1998, *Royal Scots Grey* was close to leaving Southern Region territory as it brings the returning 1S87 1210 Ramsgate-Edinburgh through Culvert Road Junction, Battersea, heading for Kensington Olympia. The 'Deltic' would work as far as Birmingham New Street before handing over to an AC electric. (Antony Guppy)

30 LOCO-HAULED - Passenger Trains of the Privatisation Era

Virgin Trains

Virgin Cross Country leased a fleet of 18 Class 86/2s to provide power for the majority of its services over the northern section of the WCML with some sharing of the fleet taking place with its sister franchise. However, appearances by EWS-owned examples were still commonplace as evidenced on June 4, 2002, as 86261 *The Rail Charter Partnership* passes Shap Beck with a southbound working. In tow is an entirely standard rake of Cross Country Mk2s with a Restaurant First Open (RFO) behind the loco, which was a rather grand designation for what was effectively a micro-buffet, followed by five TSOs and a BSO. (David Dockray)

With its Rail Express Systems paintwork in terrible condition, 86416 passes Slindon on May 12, 2001. However, the presence of the Virgin Mk3 coaches marks this out as a West Coast service rather than one for Cross Country, the 1620 Euston to Carlisle to be precise. The loco's last repaint was back in October 1992 and it would not see another, being withdrawn nine months later. (John Eyres)

The first pair of Class 47s to be officially hired to Virgin Trains by EWS were former ScotRail push-pull machines 47702 and 47711, with both being prepared for their new role in the late summer of 1998, this including an application of Virgin red/grey. However, as neither had seen an overhaul for some years, they were always temporary with withdrawal coming in the first half of 2000. On November 29, 1998, a still clean 47711 *County of Hertfordshire* was in a very unusual location for a Cross Country loco as it traverses the Great Western Main Line at Denchworth. As a result of engineering work, the 1E28 0822 Bristol Temple Meads to York had been diverted via Swindon and Oxford. (Martin Loader)

LOCO-HAULED - Passenger Trains of the Privatisation Era

Virgin Trains

A common sight around the turn of the century was a RES-liveried Class 47 atop a Cross Country set, they being the 'go to' traction from EWS if available. On August 20, 2000, 47749 *Atlantic College* leaves Bristol Temple Meads bound for Plymouth with the 0748 departure from Manchester Piccadilly, illustrating just how easy it was for the Class 47s to amass wear and tear on such lengthy diagrams. (John Eyres)

With EWS Class 47/7s so frequently employed by Cross Country, another official hire agreement was worked out with several locos also gaining Virgin colours once again. On August 27, 2001, 47747 *Graham Farish* passes through the rooftops of Manchester, having departed Oxford Road with the 1V50 0840 Glasgow Central-Penzance on its long journey to the tip of Cornwall. (John Eyres)

32 LOCO-HAULED - Passenger Trains of the Privatisation Era

Virgin Trains

The use of freight locos on Virgin Cross Country services fell into two categories, those which assisted after a failure en route and others where nothing else was available to haul the train, sometimes with a little 'help' from those in control rooms. One of the most celebrated came on June 20, 1998, when a battered 56019 took over the 1O38 0910 Edinburgh-Bournemouth at Birmingham New Street and worked through to the south coast. It duly returned on the 1M81 1814 Bournemouth to Manchester Piccadilly as far as the West Midlands with the Railfreight Red Stripe 'Grid' seen passing Culham in the last of the evening sun. (Martin Loader)

Over a year later and the 1O38 to Bournemouth was again in the hands of a freight loco, although the use of non-heat Class 47s was far more common than a Romanian-built Class 56! Heading for the seaside this time was 47348 *St Christopher's Railway Home* as it passes the south end of Oxford Hinksey Yard on August 14, 1999. The former Railfreight Distribution Type 4 would be withdrawn by EWS eight months later. (Martin Loader)

On January 12, 2001, 37606 from the European Passenger Services fleet had taken charge of the 1S87 1418 Paddington-Glasgow as far as New Street. To return the loco home, the following day saw the Type 3 'top' 47734 *Crewe Diesel Depot* on the 1O30 0717 Manchester Piccadilly-Brighton from Birmingham as far as Reading where it was detached. The odd couple are seen at Didcot East Junction nearing the end of their shared journey. (Mark Few)

LOCO-HAULED - Passenger Trains of the Privatisation Era

Virgin Trains

From a time before railway operators lost the will to undertake diversionary drags of West Coast services, the likes of the Settle & Carlisle and Glasgow & South Western played host to diesel-hauled main line trains. With a snow-covered Cross Fell in the distance, February 8, 2004, found 47757 *Capability Brown* ambling south on the S&C at Birkett Common with the 1M64 1204 Glasgow Central-Euston, which it hauled between Carlisle and Preston. This would prove to be the loco's penultimate working as on the subsequent return it expired at Blackburn, EWS duly placing it in store never to work again.
(David Dockray)

The dragging of West Coast services to Holyhead was a peculiarity of the franchise, even after the 'Pendolinos' were introduced and required Class 57/3 assistance along the North Wales coast. From a simpler time when a loco could just be hooked onto a Mk3 set, 47739 *Resourceful* powers through Mostyn on June 22, 2002, with the returning 1A62 1335 from Holyhead to Euston, which it would take as far as Crewe for an AC electric to be added to the rear.
(Terry Eyres)

34 LOCO-HAULED - Passenger Trains of the Privatisation Era

Virgin Trains

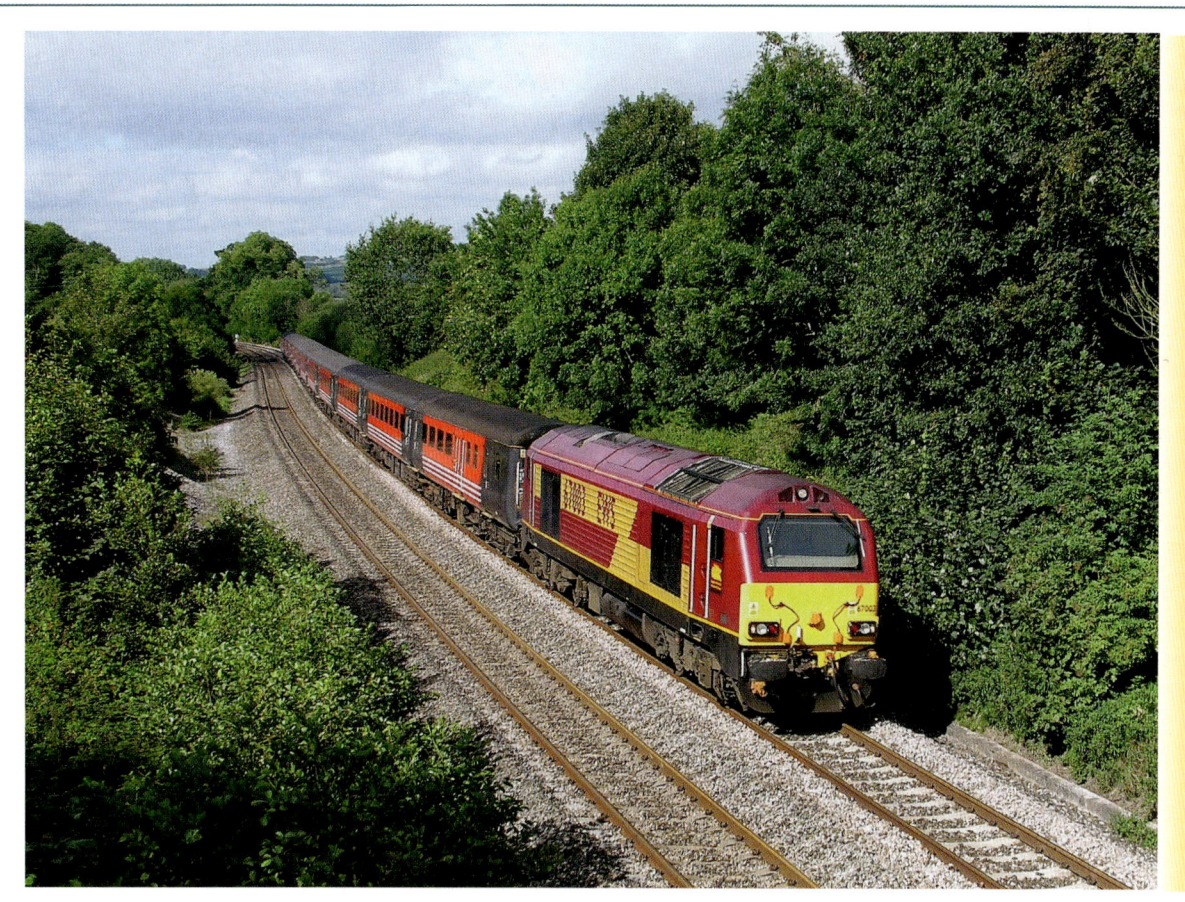

Due to the inadequacies of the 'Voyager' fleet, the summer Saturdays of 2004 saw Virgin Cross Country make a return to loco-haulage in order to give much-needed extra capacity on the busy services to and from Paignton. This involved hiring four Class 67s from EWS and the same number of ex Virgin Mk2d/e/f rakes from Riviera Trains each weekend. On August 14, 67003 makes the climb to Whiteball Tunnel with the 1E99 0905 Paignton-Preston. Sadly, the workings were not repeated in subsequent years. (John Chalcraft/Rail Photoprints)

During the second half of 2005, Virgin Cross Country introduced a push-pull set on the Birmingham New Street-Manchester Piccadilly circuit in order to take some of the strain off the stretched 'Voyagers'. While EWS provided a Class 90 along with a leased Mk3b DVT, the four Mk2f TSOs and single FO came from Riviera Trains, all of the coaches retaining unbranded Virgin colours. The diagram ceased in August 2007 in the run-up to the Arriva takeover of the Cross Country franchise. Virgin had also made use of the same formation during the autumn of 2004 to cover for the Class 220s and Class 221s while they underwent modifications. On March 23, 2006, 90018 glides through Dudley Port with a New Street to Piccadilly service. (Andy Williams)

LOCO-HAULED - Passenger Trains of the Privatisation Era

Fragonset

Pedalling to the Seaside

The early years of the 21st century saw Fragonset Railways gain two contracts to provide loco-hauled operations, these serving no less than three traditional seaside resorts. From July 2002, the company commenced a productive hire arrangement with Wessex Trains, this seeing two Class 31s and a rake of InterCity-liveried Mk2s provided to operate services to Weymouth. By the autumn, the diagram had morphed into a Fridays-only Cardiff-Brighton service, this continuing on a regular basis until September 2004.

From May 2004, Wessex Trains hired a second set of coaches from Fragonset to allow loco-haulage between Bristol Temple Meads and Weymouth to re-commence. Unmistakably finished in a pink Wessex Trains livery with Heart of Wessex brandings, the Mk2s were accompanied by similarly painted 31601. That autumn saw the train operator revert to hiring just a single set, the pink one, as it scaled back loco-hauled operations during 2005 in the run up to the end of the franchise.

Also, during 2004, First North Western hired a similar formation to act as a DMU replacement. Initially, this ran from February between the unlikely locations of St Annes and Greenbank in the morning, with a late afternoon Chester to Blackpool North return. However, this was altered from the May timetable change to a peak hours Blackpool-Manchester Victoria turn. A pair of Fragonset Class 31s was again used, sandwiching another set of Intercity Mk2s.

Class 31s returned to the southwest during the summer of 2007 to run an innovative series of trips between Bristol Temple Meads and Minehead, on the West Somerset Railway. These were intended for holidaymakers heading for the nearby Butlin's camp or Exmoor as an alternative to car or bus travel. Operated by the short-lived Victa Westlink Rail, locos and rolling stock resources from the now collapsed Fragonset Railways were employed.

In the second month of Wessex Trains employing Class 31s, the duo of 31459 *Cerberus* and 31602 *Chimaera* top and tail the 2Z87 0930 Westbury-Weymouth past the oddly named village of Queen Camel, between Castle Cary and Yeovil, on August 24, 2002. Four Mk2f TSOs, 5925/58/81 & 6168, were employed on the train with one acting as a spare, along with Mk2e BSO 9505. (Martin Loader)

Fragonset

With the transfer of the loco-hauled set to serve Brighton, this brought the very rare sight of locomotives on the Sussex Coastway line. Booked to run on Fridays only, the Class 31s could be deployed on other days if required while, equally, it was not uncommon for the set to be turned back short of its destination if running late. On December 18, 2002, 31106 *Spalding Town* and 31459 *Cerberus* had started out on the 1V94 0900 Brighton-Cardiff as they cross the River Arun at Ford, near Arundel. The coaches were through wired, enabling the blue star-equipped Type 2s to work in multiple while operating in top and tail formation. (Christopher Wilson)

During the spring of 2003, newly overhauled and reinstated 31454 was released in InterCity colours by Fragonset to match the Mk2 coaches, although for the purists it was a curious mix of the Mainline and Swallow variants. Nonetheless, the Type 2 looked rather smart on October 15 that year as it led 31602 *Chimaera*, the InterCity Mk2 set and 31468 *Hydra* as they returned to Westbury after visiting Mendip Rail's Merehead depot for fuelling. (Mark Few)

If the treatment of 31454 raised the odd eyebrow, the appearance of 31601 in a new Wessex Trains livery a year later generated apoplexy in some quarters. Supplied with five equally pink Mk2 coaches, the set allowed the passenger operator to re-introduce a loco-hauled train to Weymouth. By December 11, 2004, the loco had gained a new name of *The Mayor of Casterbridge* and is pictured at North Brewham heading the 0858 Bristol-Weymouth, which was full of Christmas shoppers. The re-liveried coaches were TSOs 6117/22/73 and BSOs 9506/25, these again featuring through wiring for multiple working. (Mark Few)

LOCO-HAULED - Passenger Trains of the Privatisation Era   37

Fragonset

The full set of five pink Mk2s, including both BSOs, brightens up an otherwise dull day in Cardiff on November 5, 2005, as 31601 at the far end and 31452 *Minotaur* depart with a service to Portsmouth. Five months later, the Wessex Trains franchise would cease to exist as it was merged with Great Western and came under the control of First Group.

Autumn had a new colour for a change as 31601 makes its presence known in the tranquil surroundings of Bradford on Avon as it crosses the aforementioned river while working the 2V74 1100 Weymouth to Bristol Temple Meads on October 25, 2004. After the end of its time on the loco-hauled duty, the loco would lose its Heart of Wessex brandings but retain the pink until late 2009, when it gained Devon & Cornwall Railway or DCR green.
(Mark Few)

Fragonset

The workings to Minehead for the Butlin's leisure park during the summer of 2007 were an interesting throwback to the holiday camp specials of the British Rail era and a valiant attempt to try something different. Run under the safety case of Victa Westlink Rail, the Class 31s and Mk2s were provided by the equally short-lived ECT Mainline Rail, which appeared on the scene following the collapse of Fragonset at the start of that year. The trains ran on Fridays, Saturdays and Mondays with August 11 seeing 31452 *Minotaur* and 31454 *The Heart of Wessex* top and tailing the 1Z35 1110 Minehead to Bristol Temple Meads 'Butlin's Express' near Flax Bourton. (Martin Loader)

During 2004, First North Western also turned to a loco-hauled solution as it struggled with a shortage of units. Initially, the afternoon working was between Chester and Blackpool North before it was changed to a more logical Blackpool to Manchester Victoria diagram. On April 22, 31459 *Cerberus* arrives at a yet to be modernised Blackpool North with the 1548 departure from Chester with 31602 *Chimaera* out of sight on the back. (John Eyres)

Some three weeks earlier, the same Brush Type 2 duo pass Ashley with the 2D44 0640 St Annes to Greenbank on March 30, which were a pair of improbable stations between which to run a hauled service. As with the Wessex operation, the InterCity Mk2s were through-wired with the TSOs employed being 5797, 5866 and 6168 (the latter having come north from the Wessex set) along with BSO 9497. (Neil Harvey)

LOCO-HAULED - Passenger Trains of the Privatisation Era **39**

East Midlands

Midland Miscellany

Unlike other parts of the country, the East Midlands was generally not the place to go for those looking for loco-haulage during the privatisation era. The only real exception to this was in 2002 when Midland Mainline opted to deploy a Class 47-hauled set to augment its HST fleet. Running between February and October, Fragonset provided a 'Brush 4' and a rake of Mk2d/e/f 'air-cons' to work a weekday morning train between Nottingham and St Pancras with another classmate taking the set north to Sheffield in the evening peak. During the train's duration, BR two-tone green liveried 47488 saw use along with Fragonset black examples 47703, 47709 and 47712.

During 2008, the still relatively new East Midlands Trains franchise hired a loco-hauled set on summer Saturdays in order to provide extra capacity on its Nottingham to Skegness services, which were always busy with day-trippers visiting the coastal resort. Provided by West Coast Railways and using mostly Mk2 air-conditioned stock, power came from top and tail Class 47s. In addition, the set spent Sunday July 20 that year shuttling back and forth between Nottingham and Grantham with 47787 and 47851 in charge, it being deployed to keep a service running during an industrial dispute,

Just over five years later, further union unrest would see East Midlands Trains again turn to loco haulage as it hired two Class 37s and Mk2s from Direct Rail Services in August 2013 to spend an afternoon and evening shuttling between Derby and Crewe. Unsurprisingly, it was packed with enthusiasts!

Standing beneath the magnificent train shed designed by William Barlow, 47709 is seen again, this time awaiting departure from St Pancras with the 1F48 1730 working to Sheffield on April 2, 2002. Normal practice was for the Class 47 that came south in the morning to be replaced by another Fragonset classmate for the trip back north, the pair swapping over again the next day. (Nigel Gibbs)

During 2002, long distance evening commuters using the Midland Main Line could travel in Mk2 comfort if desired. Three months into its operation on May 16, 2002, 47709 *Dionysos* was heading north with the 1F48 1730 St Pancras-Sheffield when it was recorded crossing the River Great Ouse and climbing the 1 in 119 gradient to Sharnbrook Summit, to the north of Bedford. (Antony Guppy)

40 LOCO-HAULED - Passenger Trains of the Privatisation Era

East Midlands

Fragonset's retro-liveried 47488 was somewhat work-stained by July 12, 2002, as it took charge of the 1B19 0932 Nottingham-St Pancras. Seen passing Wellingborough, Fragonset leased ten Mk2 coaches from HSBC Rail for the service, with seven in use here. These were RFO 1211, FO 3312, TSOs 5779/88/97 and 5812/66/88 and BSOs 9479/96, all but one having come from the former Virgin Cross Country fleet. (David Smith)

With St Pancras in the throes of rebuilding as an international station, Midland Mainline organised a special on April 8, 2004, to mark the imminent removal of intercity services from beneath the Barlow roof and into the new extension. This saw a 'Peak' return to its old stomping ground as 45112 *Royal Army Ordnance Corps* was provided to work a 1Z45 1037 departure to Leicester with Fragonset's 47355 on the rear. The 1Z46 1322 return leg to London is seen at Radwell with the loco opening up after exiting a speed restriction. (David Smith)

LOCO-HAULED - Passenger Trains of the Privatisation Era

East Midlands

Once a staple of summer Saturdays under British Rail, a loco-hauled timetabled train returned to Skegness on a few occasions in mid 2008. Provided by West Coast, the set ran for the first time on May 26 before returning again between mid July and the start of September. On July 19, 47851 *Traction Magazine* leads the 1M34 1430 Skegness-Nottingham past Great Hale Drove, to the east of Sleaford, with 47787 bringing up the rear. (Bill Atkinson)

Proving that loco workings can sometimes be fleeting in nature, the half-day of Class 37/4 haulage offered between Derby and Crewe on August 25, 2013, certainly attracted attention, and lots of it, much to the displeasure of East Midlands Trains, which had wanted the workings keep secret. With many enthusiasts and a few normal passengers crammed onto the three Mk2s, 37425 *Sir Robert McAlpine/Concrete Bob* storms out of Derby and past Litchurch Lane with the 1K05 1638 departure to Crewe. Clinging to the rear for the return leg of the DMU replacement service was 37405, the train having been hired because of an EMT guard's strike. (Terry Eyres)

42 LOCO-HAULED - Passenger Trains of the Privatisation Era

ScotRail

Shoving to Berwick

With the introduction of the 'Pendolinos' on the West Coast Main Line displacing both the Mk3s and the Driving Van Trailers (DVTs), this provided a pool of rolling stock for hire to other operators. The first to take advantage was the National Express-operated ScotRail franchise, which leased five sets of coaches, each formed of a Mk3b DVT and four Mk3a TSOs, from May 2004. These were used to replace the five Class 322s on the North Berwick to Edinburgh Waverley workings, the EMUs having been recalled to East Anglia by sister National Express franchise 'One'.

Powered by Class 90s from the EWS fleet and working in push-pull formation, the Mk3s remained in Virgin colours but most eventually gained silver ScotRail logos. Their use came to an end in September 2005 after new franchisee First ScotRail negotiated the return of the Class 322s.

The North Berwick workings are certainly a strong contender for the most bizarre loco-hauled service of the privatisation era. On May 20, 2005, 90037 *Spirit of Dagenham* had recently arrived at North Berwick, and more or less fitted in the platform, with the 2Y10 1034 from Edinburgh Waverley. Nestled in between flats, houses and a car park, the tiny terminus station had never seen anything like it but at least there was a sea view to enjoy. (Kevin Machin)

Once off the North Berwick branch, there was a short blast along the East Coast Main Line into Edinburgh, albeit with the need to stop at the five intermediate stations along the way. On August 30, 2005, and just before the Class 90s departed from the workings, 90021 was only a short way into its journey along the single track branch as it passes Fenton Barns with the 2Y01 1217 North Berwick-Edinburgh. (Scott Borthwick)

LOCO-HAULED - Passenger Trains of the Privatisation Era 43

Arriva Northern

Tractors
Over the Top

As part of a plan to offer an improved service over the Settle & Carlisle line, September 2003 saw Arriva Trains Northern commence a 12-month experimental loco-hauled operation. Encompassing a return trip over the scenic route from Leeds to Carlisle, there was also a peak hours fill-in turn between Leeds and Knaresborough.

Booked for top and tail haulage by two EWS Class 37/4s, 37405, 37408 and 37411 were the normal locos but substitutions by other sub-classes were not uncommon, especially in the summer of 2004. A pool of six Mk2f coaches was made available, TSOs 6035/66 and 6124/70 along with BSOs 9521/24, these all being blue star through-wired to allow the locos to work together and painted in Arriva turquoise with white doors. Sadly, the workings ceased at the end of September 2004 in preparation for the commencement of the new Northern Rail franchise.

Pictured at one of the classic locations on the S&C, 37408 *Loch Rannoch* is in charge as it climbs to Ais Gill summit on September 9, 2004, in the last month of operation for the loco-hauled set. With 37411 for company, the working was the 1E23 1333 Carlisle-Leeds. In due course, the Mk2f coaches would move to South Wales and join the Rhymney pool. (Bill Atkinson)

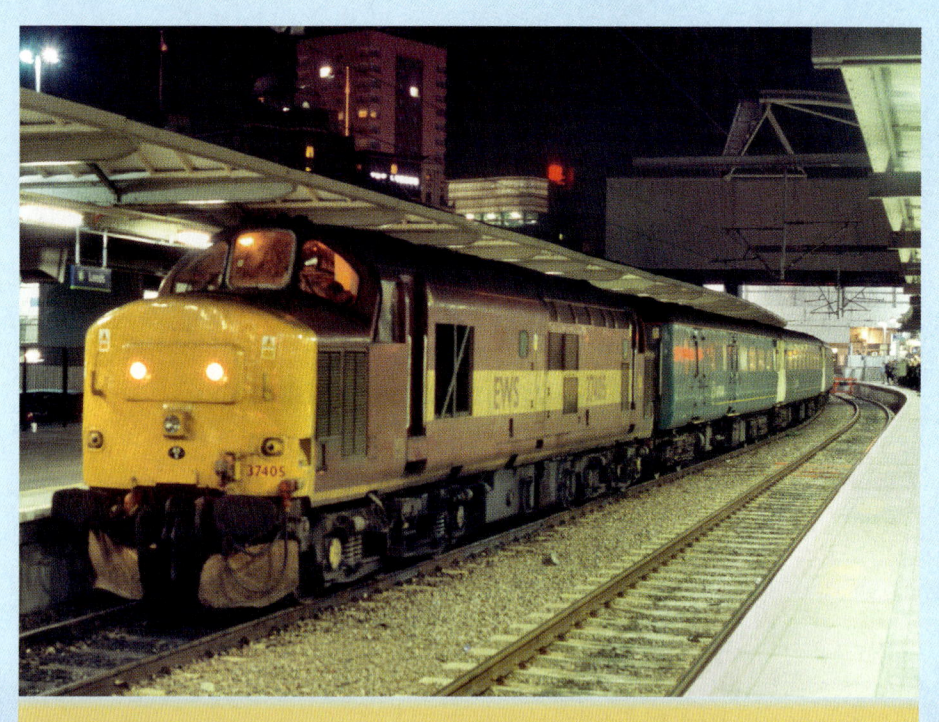

Not all of the loco-hauled duty was undertaken in such scenery though as 37405 awaits departure from the distinctly urban surroundings of Leeds on November 27, 2003, with the 2C72 1743 Leeds to Knaresborough part of the diagram. (Neil Harvey)

Arriva Northern

Even in the spring, the Settle & Carlisle line can be a cold place to be so the train heating being supplied by 37411 *The Scottish Railway Preservation Society* on March 1, 2004, would doubtless have been appreciated by the passengers on the 1E23 1333 Carlisle-Leeds. Seen crossing Ais Gill Viaduct, 37405 was on the rear while the four Mk2f coaches, three TSO and a BSO, were the standard formation. (Dave McAlone)

With autumn starting to take effect on October 17, 2003, the 1M53 0947 Leeds to Carlisle dodges the clouds at Smardale with 37405 bringing up the rear of the train as 37408 *Loch Rannoch* leads the way north. The 12-month trial was a commendable one by Arriva Trains Northern, enabling units to be released for use elsewhere as well as allowing passengers to enjoy the delights of the line from a 'proper' train. (Jimmy Wilson)

LOCO-HAULED - Passenger Trains of the Privatisation Era

Open Access

East Coast Substitutes

December 2007 saw Grand Central commence its open access operation between Sunderland and King's Cross using its newly refurbished HST sets. However, the company soon found that its six power cars were far from up to the job of pounding the East Coast Main Line after a period in store. While they were dispatched in turn to Brush Traction for rectification, the company was forced to bring in loco-hauled replacements from April 2008 in order to maintain a reduced service.

Hiring a rake of Riviera coaches and then a set of EWS-owned Mk2 'air-cons', these were initially teamed with a pair of Class 67s and continued to operate through to London. However, issues with the traction allowed by Grand Central's safety case meant that the General Motors locos could not be used again when the loco-hauled set returned for a second and longer spell at the end of May.

With the use of EWS Class 37/4s also ruled out, the operator turned to Riviera Trains for a month long hire of Class 47s. An amended timetable was also put in place with the loco-hauled set restricted to working between Sunderland and York, where it connected with an HST for onward journeys to London. With the paperwork allowing the use of the Brush Type 4s also expiring in mid June, Class 57/3s hired from Virgin Trains were next up on the train, although these only worked for a week before enough HST power cars were once again available.

The other East Coast open access operator, Hull Trains, also hit trouble in January 2007 after one of its Class 222 'Pioneer' sets was badly damaged in a lifting accident; a partial failure of a set of synchronised jacks seeing one car come down while still securely attached to the next. For the next 12 months, Hull continued to operate its services using its remaining sets but with full utilisation required, this gave little time for more involved maintenance.

As a result, a Mk3 push-pull rake was drafted in as a replacement from January 2008, pending the arrival of a Class 180 'Adelante' that April. Operating between King's Cross and Doncaster at weekends only, the AC Loco Group's 86101 provided power for a short rake of Cargo-D coaches and Porterbrook-owned DVT 82115, the latter looking most unusual repainted in all over BR blue.

Shortly after its launch at the end of 2007, Grand Central faced a crisis as its overhauled HST power cars proved not to be up to scratch and unable to cope with high speed running without frequent failures. While they were sent in turn to Brush Traction for the job to be done properly, a hauled set was drafted in as cover. With Class 67s initially hired, these were able to run the full route from Sunderland to London without much difficultly. On April 22, 67020 and 67003 thunder south at Bridge 33, south of Colton Junction, with the 1A63 1730 Sunderland-King's Cross, the Mk2s coming from EWS' own charter fleet.
(Neil Harvey)

Open Access

The frustrations of the privatised railway then came into play as paperwork prevented Grand Central from using the EWS machines for a second time when the substitute stock needed to return for a second and longer period in May and June 2008. As a result, Class 47s had to be brought in from Riviera Trains and a Sunderland to York shuttle introduced as the Type 4s would not be able to keep to the 100mph timings on the ECML. On June 13, 47853 *Rail Express* leads the way with the 1Z26 1444 York-Sunderland at Dawdon on the Durham coast with 47839 in support. After a four-week period, the Class 47s then had to be briefly replaced by Class 57/3s, again due to safety case restrictions, but by then enough rectified power cars were available to allow full HST operation to resume. (Jimmy Wilson)

For just over three months at the beginning of 2008, 86101 *Sir William A Stanier FRS* could be found plying the southern half of the ECML at weekends on hire to Hull Trains. On Sundays, the push-pull set would work north from King's Cross to Doncaster with DVT 82115 leading before it returned as empty stock to Bounds Green. While a somewhat wasteful operation, this gave an opportunity to photograph the Class 86 at the head of the set and, if lucky, with the sun on it. Such was the case on January 27 as the 5G02 1233 Doncaster-Bounds Green heads south at Marston, near Grantham. (Bill Atkinson)

LOCO-HAULED - Passenger Trains of the Privatisation Era   47

Great Western

Saturdays to Weekdays

During the summers of 2007/08, First Great Western (FGW) provided loco-haulage on Saturdays only between Bristol Temple Meads and Weymouth to bolster capacity on the route. Operated by pairs of Class 67s, Riviera Trains provided a rake of former Virgin Trains Mk2 'air-cons'. From December 2008, FGW expanded this operation to a weekdays-only diagram between Taunton and Cardiff, this being introduced due to a shortage of DMUs caused by the transfer back to Northern Rail of a number of Class 142s that had been on loan. The EWS/DB Type 5s again officiated, this time with Cargo-D blue/grey and EWS maroon Mk2s. Initially envisaged as a short-term solution while cascaded Class 150s were awaited, in the event FGW was required to operate loco-hauled sets for just under two years due to delays in constructing the new Class 172 'Turbostars'. From May 2009, this set also saw use on the summer-dated trains to Weymouth.

From December 2009, a second loco-hauled set was introduced as First GBRf took over the Taunton-Cardiff diagram using a pair of Class 57/3s and Riviera Mk2s. The latter were all Anglia-liveried examples, minus brandings, with Mk2f BSO 9520 being repainted to provide a matching brake vehicle, while spare Mk2s in InterCity colours were also made available. A replacement spare set would be provided in February 2010, this again being all Anglia vehicles with another repainted BSO in the form of 9527. The Class 57/3s were drawn from the common IWCA pool, meaning that Arriva liveried examples were not unknown in the early days of the service, although those still in Virgin Trains colours were by far the most dominant. Meanwhile, the existing Class 67 set moved onto a new Cardiff-Paignton diagram from the same month, this still operating with Cargo-D and EWS/DB Mk2s.

First Great Western brought loco-haulage back to Weymouth on summer Saturdays during the second half of the 2000s. Pictured during the second season of this on July 12, 2008, the passengers on the 1655 Weymouth to Bristol Temple Meads could pretend to be royalty just for one day as the train featured both claret Class 67s. Seen on the approach to Bath, 67006 *Royal Sovereign* was leading the way with 67005 *Queen's Messenger* in tow. The Riviera and former Virgin Mk2s do not quite compare to the Royal train though! (John Chalcraft/Rail Photoprints)

Great Western

However, the Class 57/3s proved to be less than reliable performers as 2010 wore on, leading to substitutions by First GBRf Class 66s on occasions. By the start of July, First Great Western's patience had worn out, it terminating the contract of the newly sold off GB Railfreight and ending the use of the 'Thunderbirds.' In their place came a second pair of Class 67s, these seeing use with both the Anglia and InterCity Mk2s from Riviera. Once again, summer Saturdays in 2010 brought an out and back working to Weymouth, this initially using a pair of Class 67s before the condition of the track saw Network Rail impose a restriction of just one. With the arrival of additional DMUs, the Paignton diagram ceased in October 2010 with the Taunton ending a month later.

First Great Western next turned to loco haulage in the summer of 2014 with a Saturdays-only diagram between Par and Exeter with a return working through to Penzance. Resourced from its own rolling stock for a change, the service employed the seated vehicles from the Night Riviera sleeper powered by a Class 57 and running as either three or four coach formations. These trains ran for the next four summers as well, during which time First Great Western became Great Western Railway but did not return for the 2019 season as the refurbished 'Castle' HSTs took their place.

While most of these workings featured the operator's own Class 57/6s, at times Class 57/3s from the DRS fleet took charge. One of the latter had been on hire to the franchise since 2014 to help provide resilience at a time when the home fleet was going through a period of poor reliability and overhauls. This hire continued in mid-2020, albeit with the loco typically used for EMU transfers and empty stock moves.

During the summer of 2009, the Weymouth diagram operated once again with Class 67s this time partnered with a mix of blue/grey Cargo-D and EWS maroon Mk2s. At the time, it was thought that this would be the last season that loco-hauled trains reached the Dorset coast so for the final Saturday, September 5, the English Electric duo of 37670 *St Blazey T&RS Depot* and 37401 were specially rostered, these pretty much being DB Schenker's last operational Class 37s. With a strengthened set of coaches in tow, the duo thrash past Bathampton with the outbound 2O72 0909 Bristol Temple Meads-Weymouth. (Charles Woodland)

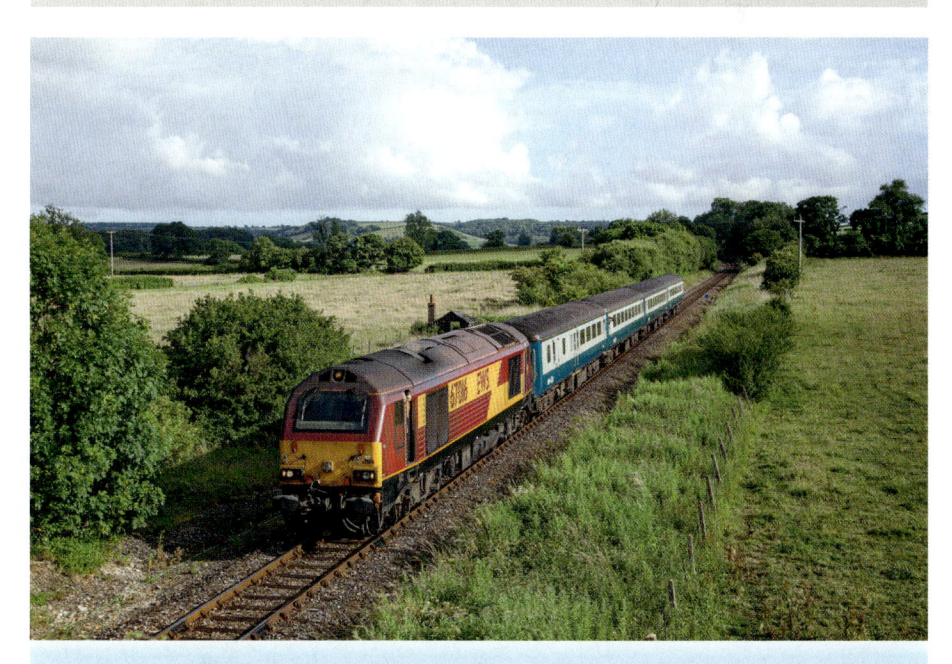

In the event, it was 2010 that saw the demise of the summer Saturday workings to Weymouth as First Great Western finally received extra DMUs. Depicting the more typical look of these services at the time, 67016 is seen leading a late running 2V67 1655 Weymouth-Bristol north at Chetnole on July 3 with the standard load of four Mk2s. The season had begun with top and tailed Type 5s but the poor condition of the track led Network Rail to decree that only one loco could be sent from mid-June due to concerns about the impact of their heavy axle loadings. (Jonathan Lewis)

LOCO-HAULED - Passenger Trains of the Privatisation Era

Great Western

Throughout 2009, a Class 67-powered set had been deployed on the Taunton to Cardiff circuit to help cope with the unit shortage. From December 2009 and throughout the first half of 2010, this was taken over by Class 57/3s and Riviera stock, mostly in the former Anglia Railways colours as this served as a useful neutral livery. Resourced by First GBRf, as it was at the time, June 4, 2010, found 57308 *Tin Tin* and 57305 *John Tracy* partnered together to work the 0728 Taunton-Bristol Parkway as they approached Temple Meads at Parson Street. (John Chalcraft/Rail Photoprints)

Unfortunately, the Class 57/3s were not up to the task with numerous reliability problems, although this was perhaps not a surprise given the locos went from sitting around not doing much to an intensive diagram with much stopping and starting. To provide cover, occasionally First GBRf drafted in its Class 66s, including the former DRS example 66402. On June 28, 2010, and with 57308 as a partner, they had already worked from Bristol Parkway to Weston-Super-Mare and were now performing a 5Y10 1010 empty stock move to Taunton prior to forming the 2U14 1102 Taunton-Cardiff. The GM would become 66734 a year later, only to suffer a premature end after hitting a landslide and derailing alongside Loch Treig in June 2012, it having to be dismantled on site the following summer after recovery proved impossible. (Christopher Perkins)

50 LOCO-HAULED - Passenger Trains of the Privatisation Era

Great Western

By the summer of 2010, First Great Western had lost patience with the Class 57/3s and terminated GB Railfreight's contract, a process no doubt made easier by the freight company having just been sold by First Group to Europorte. In their place came a second Class 67 set and this is seen in its first week of deployment on July 9, 2010, with 67018 *Keith Heller* and 67029 *Royal Diamond* either end of a Riviera set of Mk2s. The duo was powering the 2C79 1400 Cardiff-Taunton when pictured at Patchway. (Mark Few)

While the Taunton diagram was beset by drama, the first Class 67 set had moved onto a new Cardiff-Paignton duty from December 2009 and ran pretty much with incident during 2010 until it ceased that October. On April 27, 67017 *Arrow* and 67022 head for the Severn Tunnel as they pass Pilning with the 2U20 1247 Paignton to Cardiff Central. Along with 67016, 67017 became a regular on the FGW duties and the pair were inseparable for a long time, so much so that they were nicknamed Andy and Lou after the characters from the popular *Little Britain* television sketch show. (Martin Loader)

LOCO-HAULED - Passenger Trains of the Privatisation Era 51

Great Western

Returning to the Weymouth line, the very last and final FGW loco-hauled working to the Dorset coast occurred on September 4, 2010. While the motive power was more General Motors than English Electric this time around, the event was at least marked by the special rostering of 57604 *Pendennis Castle.* The GWR-liveried machine is captured looking the part as it brings the returning 2V67 1655 Weymouth-Bristol Temple Meads through Thornford. (Charles Woodland)

It may have taken seven years, but a hauled set returned to Weymouth, albeit as a one-off, on June 3, 2017. With the UEFA Champions League final taking place in Cardiff that evening, an HST could not be spared for the Weymouth diagram, leading to the hiring of DB's 67010 to work the 1O72 0906 Bristol Temple Meads-Weymouth, which is seen at Avoncliff. With 11 Mk2s in tow, it was the longest timetabled passenger train seen on the route since the British Rail era. However, these were not specifically intended for Weymouth passengers as, following the 1V72 return to Bristol, 67010 continued to Cardiff to take up 'footex' duties, first working back to Temple Meads before departing from Cardiff after midnight bound for Paddington. (Mark Few)

52 LOCO-HAULED - Passenger Trains of the Privatisation Era

Great Western

Away from the Dorset, Avon and Somerset area and going back further in time, First Great Western had employed hired-in motive power before. Just like Virgin Cross Country, FGW's small fleet of Class 47s were somewhat temperamental at the start of this century, leading it to first call on Fragonset for assistance. At this time, a small number of daytime loco-hauled trains still existed as there were insufficient HSTs available, although this would change as the Virgin sets were released. On September 29, 2001, Fragonset-operated but privately-owned 47701 *Waverley* passes through Torre station with the Saturdays-only 1C23 1033 Paddington-Paignton 'Torbay Express'. (Mark Few)

By 2006, FGW's own Class 47 fleet had long since departed and the rebuilt Class 57/6s were in charge of the only remaining hauled trains, the Night Riviera sleepers. However, when these suffered their own period of poor availability, it was Cotswold Rail that aided with the return of Brush-built machines still featuring a Sulzer engine. On July 23, 2006, 47813 *John Peel* stands on the blocks at Paddington, having brought the sleeper empty stock in from Old Oak Common. At the other end, silver sister 47828 *Joe Strummer* would take the train to Penzance. (Richard Stiles)

LOCO-HAULED - Passenger Trains of the Privatisation Era 53

Great Western

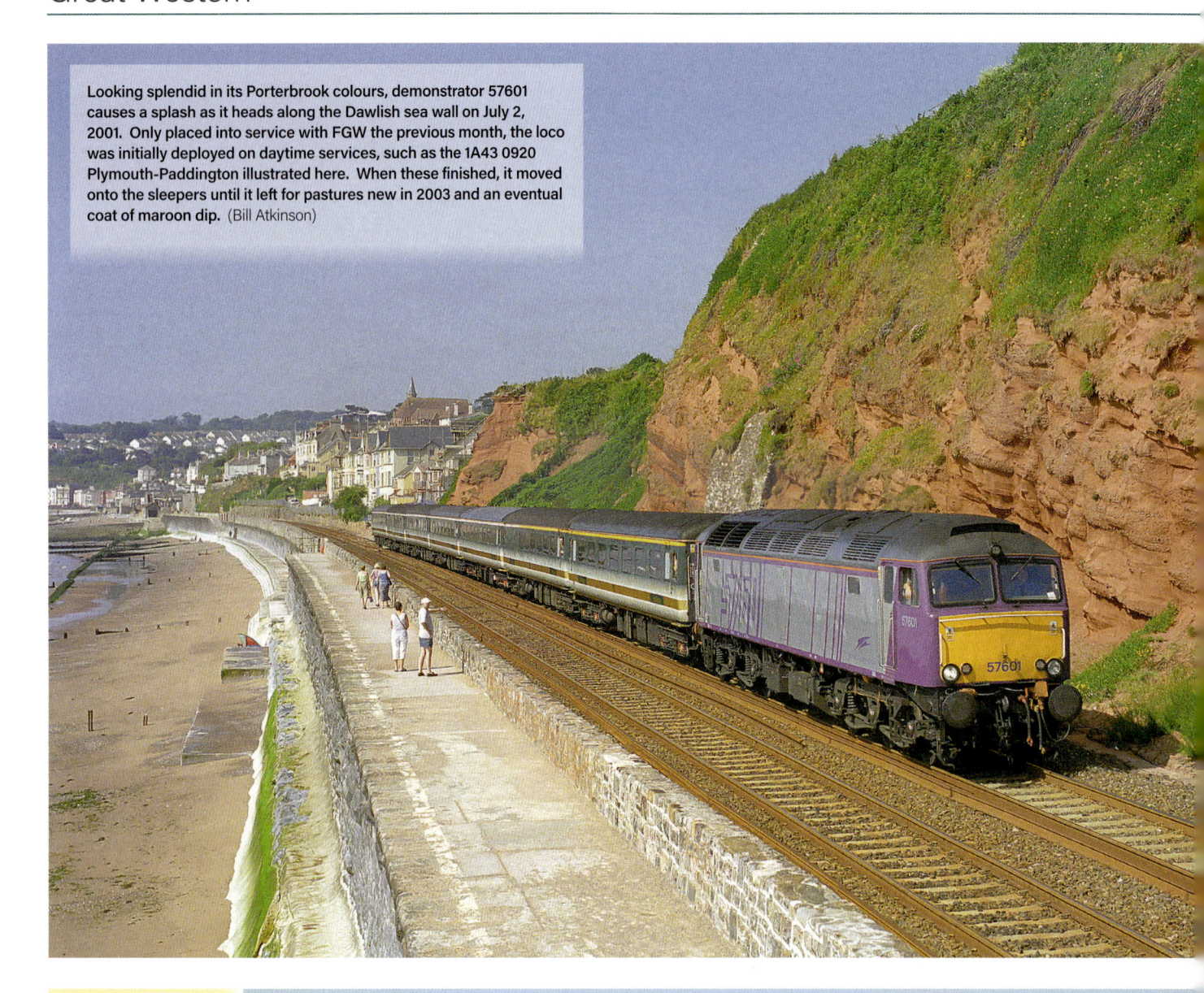

Looking splendid in its Porterbrook colours, demonstrator 57601 causes a splash as it heads along the Dawlish sea wall on July 2, 2001. Only placed into service with FGW the previous month, the loco was initially deployed on daytime services, such as the 1A43 0920 Plymouth-Paddington illustrated here. When these finished, it moved onto the sleepers until it left for pastures new in 2003 and an eventual coat of maroon dip. (Bill Atkinson)

The daytime summer Saturday Class 57 diagram commenced in 2014, the same year that First Great Western began to hire an additional loco from DRS. One of the first to be employed was 57305, this still retaining its Network Rail livery. Late on September 5 that year, the loco took charge of the 1C99 2345 Paddington-Penzance Night Riviera, putting it in position to work the 2E75 1125 Par to Exeter St Davids the next morning. The yellow peril is seen crossing Lynher Viaduct, St Germans, but the return leg would be cancelled after an electric train supply fault developed, the stock returning empty to Penzance. (Daniel Phillips)

Great Western

Despite its shiny Northern Belle livery, which had only been applied four months earlier, even 57312 had a stint with FGW, albeit a brief one. Doing the job largely intended for the hired in DRS loco, *Solway Princess* stands at Paddington early on January 20, 2015, waiting to drag the 5A40 empty sleeper stock to Old Oak Common for servicing. (Daniel Phillips)

In perfect evening sun, 57303 *Pride of Carlisle* powers away from the station stop at Dawlish Warren with the 2C51 1750 Exeter St Davids to Penzance on July 11, 2015. With the adoption of the new Great Western Railway brand and the associated green livery in progress, the Mk3 set is formed of two Brake First Opens (BFO) along with a TSO and a buffet. (Nathan Williamson)

LOCO-HAULED - Passenger Trains of the Privatisation Era 55

East Anglia

Diesels in the Broads

By the mid-1990s, the long association of East Anglia with diesel-hauled passenger trains had been severely curtailed, firstly by the completion of electrification to Norwich from London Liverpool Street in 1987 and then the similar wiring of Cambridge and King's Lynn in 1990 and 1992 respectively. The introduction of 'Sprinters' had a similar effect on cross-country services in ousting diesel locos.

However, there was still one area of the region that could be pretty much guaranteed to bring out a variety of diesel traction and that was the additional summer weekend services to the coastal towns of Great Yarmouth and Lowestoft, where passenger demand would otherwise overwhelm regular workings. Right from the start of privatisation, the shadow Anglia franchise hired Class 31/4s from EWS for this purpose in 1996 and this continued under the control of Anglia Railways from the following year. This included bringing in Class 47s from Fragonset, EWS and even Freightliner through to 2002 along with, briefly, the unlikely duo of D9000 and 50050 from Deltic 9000 Locomotives Ltd.

Some stability was achieved from 2002 as Cotswold Rail appeared on the scene with its varied and expanding fleet of Class 47s. Anglia Railways gave way to National Express from April 2004, this initially being under the much derided 'One' brand, with Cotswold handed the job of catering for all of the franchise's diesel traction needs, be it 'Thunderbird' standby duties, summer workings to the coast, stock transfers or other ad-hoc jobs.

The summer of 2009 saw Direct Rail Services oust Cotswold Rail as the diesel traction supplier of choice to National Express. Initially charged with hauling the famed summer Saturday drags of AC electrics to Great Yarmouth, DRS was further tasked with providing traction for a loco-hauled DMU replacement during February 2010. Running for much of the month, the short set consisted of just two Mk3s and a DVT, the latter acting as a brake vehicle, and running between Norwich and Great Yarmouth/ Lowestoft. Besides a single day's appearance by 20304 and a few outings for 57004, the duty was solidly covered by DRS Class 47s. This formation returned late in June 2011 as National Express struggled with a shortage of DMUs. Again operating between Norwich and the two seaside towns, it was solidly powered by Class 47s with 47501, 47712 and 47802/810/818/841 all seeing use before the duty ended that December.

Prior to the Anglia operation passing into private hands, 31407 departs Acle with the 1135 service from Norwich to Great Yarmouth on September 7, 1996. This was unique amongst the Class 31s in carrying the attractive Mainline Freight livery while the Mk2s coaches taken from the InterCity fleet were standing in for a unit in order to increase capacity. This summer also saw 'Dutch' grey/yellow-liveried 31466 employed as well. (Richard Norris)

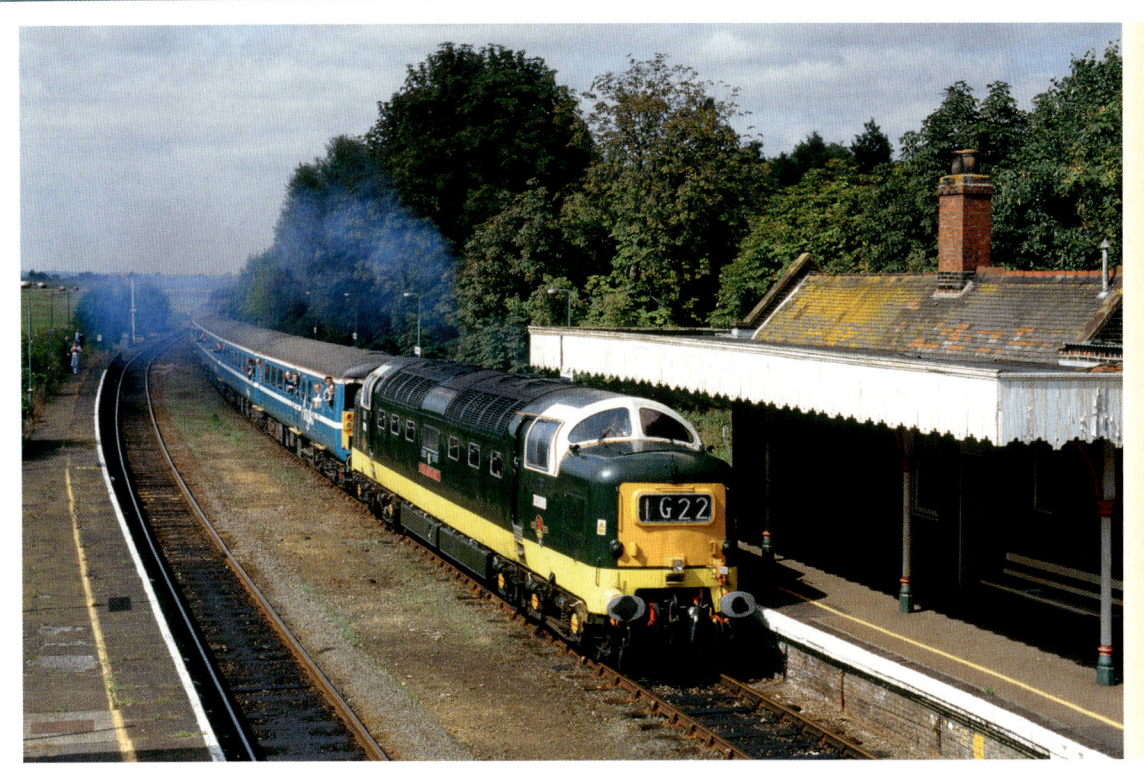

East Anglia

The hiring of 'Deltic' D9000 *Royal Scots Grey* by Anglia Railways for use on a service train on August 31, 1998, was certainly novel, it bringing the first visit of one of the mighty machines to the Norfolk coast. Packed full of enthusiasts with even more lineside, the Type 5 powers through Reedham on what was planned to be a non-stop run with the 1G22 1055 Liverpool Street-Great Yarmouth. A full rake of newly repainted and refurbished Anglia coaches was deliberately provided due to the publicity the working would receive, a prediction that unsurprisingly came true! (Martin Loader)

The Rail Express Systems Class 47 fleet, by now owned by EWS, were a common sight in East Anglia around the turn of the century working the Norwich to Great Yarmouth 'drags'. On July 18, 1998, 86237 *University of East Anglia* had worked from London to Norwich with the remainder of its journey to the coast taking place behind 47778 *Duke of Edinburgh's Award*, the location being Whittlingham Junction. (Gareth Bayer)

The Saturdays of summer 1999 saw 50050 *Fearless* deployed on Norwich to Yarmouth workings on several occasions. Although privately-owned, the 'Hoover' was under the stewardship of Deltic 9000 Locomotives Ltd at this time and is seen departing Norwich on July 3, 1999. In tow is a scratch set of Mk2s, including a DBSO in use as a brake coach. (Gareth Bayer)

Long before the term 'short set' had become trendy, RES-liveried 47789 *Lindisfarne* leads a DMU replacement working past Breydon Water on April 8, 2002. Bringing up the rear is Fragonset-operated 47701 *Waverley* with the 2P28 1233 Norwich-Great Yarmouth being formed of three TSOs and a BSO, the latter on hire to Anglia. The leading pair of TSOs is also notable, being two of the high-density seating conversions from former first class vehicles. (Anthony Kay)

LOCO-HAULED - Passenger Trains of the Privatisation Era   57

East Anglia

The advent of the Abellio-operated Greater Anglia franchise in February 2012 brought no improvement in DMU availability so the Class 47-powered 'short set', as it was now universally dubbed, was reluctantly returned to the Norwich-Lowestoft/Great Yarmouth circuit once more between March and April that year. The company then managed to do without it for a further 12 months but the set was reformed on a more permanent basis in April 2013 and remained in use throughout the rest of the year and into 2014. Still formed of two Mk3s and a DVT sandwiched between DRS Class 47s, this formation remained unchanged until the middle of June 2014.

From this date, DRS' own Mk2f coaches were introduced to replace the Mk3s, the set now consisting of two TSOs and a BSO, while the top and tailed Class 47s were also shown the door in favour of English Electric Type 3s from June 2015. Thereafter, the Class 37s ruled on the 'short set', always working in top and tail form after initial plans to introduce push-pull working with a Mk2f DBSO were dropped. A second loco-hauled set was also brought in between July 2016 and September 2017 as unit availability dropped further, this using a pair of Class 68s and Mk2s hired from Riviera Trains. The last two years were all about the 'Tractors' in their various colourful forms but, sadly, the fun came to an end in September 2019 as the new Stadler 'Flirt' units were introduced.

For eight weeks in the summer of 2004, Network Rail imposed a total blockade at Ipswich in order to perform gauge clearance work inside Ipswich Tunnel to allow 9ft 6in tall containers to pass through. Among the many alternative travel arrangements was the diversion of a small number of Liverpool Street to Norwich services via Cambridge, these requiring diesel assistance between Cambridge and Norwich. On July 27, Cotswold Rail's 47813 was still carrying First Great Western green as it powers through the Breckland scenery near Thetford atop the 1G24 1147 Liverpool Street-Norwich with 86230 on the rear. (Gareth Bayer)

The Ipswich blockade ran between July 11 and September 5, 2004, this being during the time National Express was replacing its venerable Class 86 fleet with Class 90s displaced from Virgin Trains. However, on August 17, an all Anglia Railways formation was recorded at Thetford making up the 1G49 1212 Norwich-Liverpool Street with 47714 topping 86238 *European Community* as far as Cambridge. The Type 4 had received the Anglia colours in September 2003 and still retained them 17 years later in 2020, albeit nowhere near as smart as it appears here. (Gareth Bayer)

East Anglia

With National Express having taken over the Anglia franchise two months earlier, Cotswold Rail continued to provide diesel traction as required as seen on June 6, 2004, as 47200 *The Fosse Way* arrives at Reedham with the 1G56 1225 Norwich to Great Yarmouth. The silver Type 4 initially saw considerable use in East Anglia alongside sister 47316 but both were later pushed aside as Cotswold acquired more useful class members fitted with electric train supply.
(Steve Goodrum)

A different view of Reedham on July 30, 2004, shows how coast-bound services were strengthened around summer weekends. Newly repainted in 'One' colours, 47818 is seen departing with the 1G56 1225 Norwich-Yarmouth once again, the service having originated from Liverpool Street and consequently formed of a full Mk2 set. Barely visible on the rear is 47316 *Cam Peak* while heading in the opposite direction were Class 170 'Turbostars' 170203 and 170273, these returning empty to Norwich.
(Gareth Bayer)

Previously part of the Fragonset fleet, 47703 was a Cotswold Rail machine by the time it was photographed nearing Reedham on a misty September 22, 2007. With the Yarmouth 'drags' coming to an end for another year, the former ScotRail machine was in charge of the 1V29 1008 departure from the coast to Norwich and ultimately London. In tow is a full set of Mk3 coaches in 'One' colours with 90008 on the rear for the later journey to Liverpool Street.
(Gareth Bayer)

LOCO-HAULED - Passenger Trains of the Privatisation Era 59

East Anglia

Once a fixture of the summer season, the annual airshow at Lowestoft saw services to the town strengthened across the weekend to cope with demand. On July 25, 2008, Advenza Freight-liveried 47375 was in charge of such an additional working to the seaside as it approaches Haddiscoe with 47818 on the rear. By this date, National Express had abandoned the 'One' identity in favour of a more corporate look with the Mk3s having already lost their rainbow stripes and the application of replacement white bands in progress. (John Chalcraft/ Rail Photoprints)

The 2008 summer season was the last year of Cotswold Rail's involvement with the Yarmouth 'drags'. On August 30 that year, a smokey 47813 *John Peel* heads 90004 on the 1V26 1418 Norwich-Great Yarmouth at Stracey Arms The Type 4 had already had an eventful day, first taking 90015 and its train to and from the coast before recovering a disabled 90009 from Diss after it struck debris on the track while working to Norwich. Now attached to its third Class 90 of the day, the train would later work back empty to Crown Point depot. (Bill Atkinson)

East Anglia

By the following year, Direct Rail Services had been installed as the provider of diesel traction to National Express East Anglia. On the very first 'drag' of the 2009 season, 47832 *Solway Princess* brings the 5V29 0840 Norwich Crown Point-Great Yarmouth empty stock move into its destination on May 23. Once the Class 47 had run round, this would head back to Norwich as the 1V29 1008 departure and onwards to Liverpool Street behind 90008. Although the AC electric and its Mk3 set are fully finished in National Express colours, the application of the company's corporate livery progressed little further. (Bill Atkinson)

Moving forward to 2014, this was the last year of the AC electric 'drags' but this was not confirmed until after they had concluded for the summer. On July 26, 47805 *John Scott 12.5.45-22.5.12* traverses Reedham Junction with the 1V43 1310 Great Yarmouth to Norwich and Liverpool Street with 90003 on the back. By this date, the franchise had been under Abellio control for over two years with the application of the Greater Anglia livery well underway. (Steve Goodrum)

LOCO-HAULED - Passenger Trains of the Privatisation Era 61

East Anglia

For many years, the Anglia franchise under its various operators often struggled for DMUs due to the small size of the fleet. Any out of course incident put further pressure on availability but with numerous level and farm crossings in the region, collisions with road vehicles were inevitable due to driver misuse. When a Class 156 suffered considerable damage in such an incident, National Express East Anglia was forced to run a loco-hauled replacement throughout the second half of 2011, having already briefly used such a set-up a year earlier. On July 22, 47802 *Pride of Cumbria* rumbles through Brundall Gardens with the 2P33 1817 Great Yarmouth to Norwich, 47841 being on the rear. While the inclusion of a DVT was somewhat wasteful in terms of seating, it was required to provide guard's accommodation and a parking brake. (Steve Goodrum)

From the spring of 2013, Greater Anglia reinstated a loco-hauled diagram between Norwich and Yarmouth/Lowestoft on a rolling basis, one that lasted for over six years. Initially using DRS Class 47s and Mk3s, the coaches were replaced by Mk2s in the summer of 2014. A year later, on June 15, 2015, the Type 4s were also about to be ousted as 47813 *Solent* tails the 2P32 1736 Norwich-Yarmouth through Beighton with 47818 leading. (Steve Goodrum)

The new order in the form of Class 37s is seen near Haddiscoe on September 10, 2015, as 37419 *Carl Haviland 1954-2012* heads up the 2J80 1455 Norwich-Lowestoft with 37405 on the rear. Plans to introduce push-pull working with a Mk2f DBSO never got beyond the planning stage, quite possibly due to the poor reliability that was then being encountered on the Cumbrian coast operation. (Bill Atkinson)

East Anglia

For 14 months between the summers of 2016/17, Greater Anglia brought in a second hauled set to provide further capacity enhancements. Somewhat surprisingly, Class 68s were specified for this formation despite the considerable cost of hiring the multi-million pound traction. On August 28, 2017, 68005 *Defiant* and 68028 top and tail the 2J81 1457 Lowestoft-Norwich past infrastructure of an altogether different age at Reedham. (Phil Chilton)

After another day of English Electric action over the Norfolk Broads, the evening begins to draw in as 37424 *Avro Vulcan XH558* sets out from Great Yarmouth once more with the 2P29 1717 departure to Norwich on September 1, 2018, with 37405 for company. The decision by DRS to repaint several of its Class 37/4s into BR large logo blue as a 'neutral' colour scheme further contributed to the appeal of the East Anglia workings with enthusiasts drawn from across the country to sample and photograph them. (Phil Chilton)

LOCO-HAULED - Passenger Trains of the Privatisation Era

East Anglia

Earlier on September 1, 2018, it was 37405's turn to take the lead with 37424 on the rear as the duo takes the 2C52 0955 Norwich-Great Yarmouth past Lockgate Drainage Mill. One of the lesser photographed locations on the route, this may have something to do with it being around a 50 minute walk each way but one that captures the nature of the Broads perfectly. (Phil Chilton)

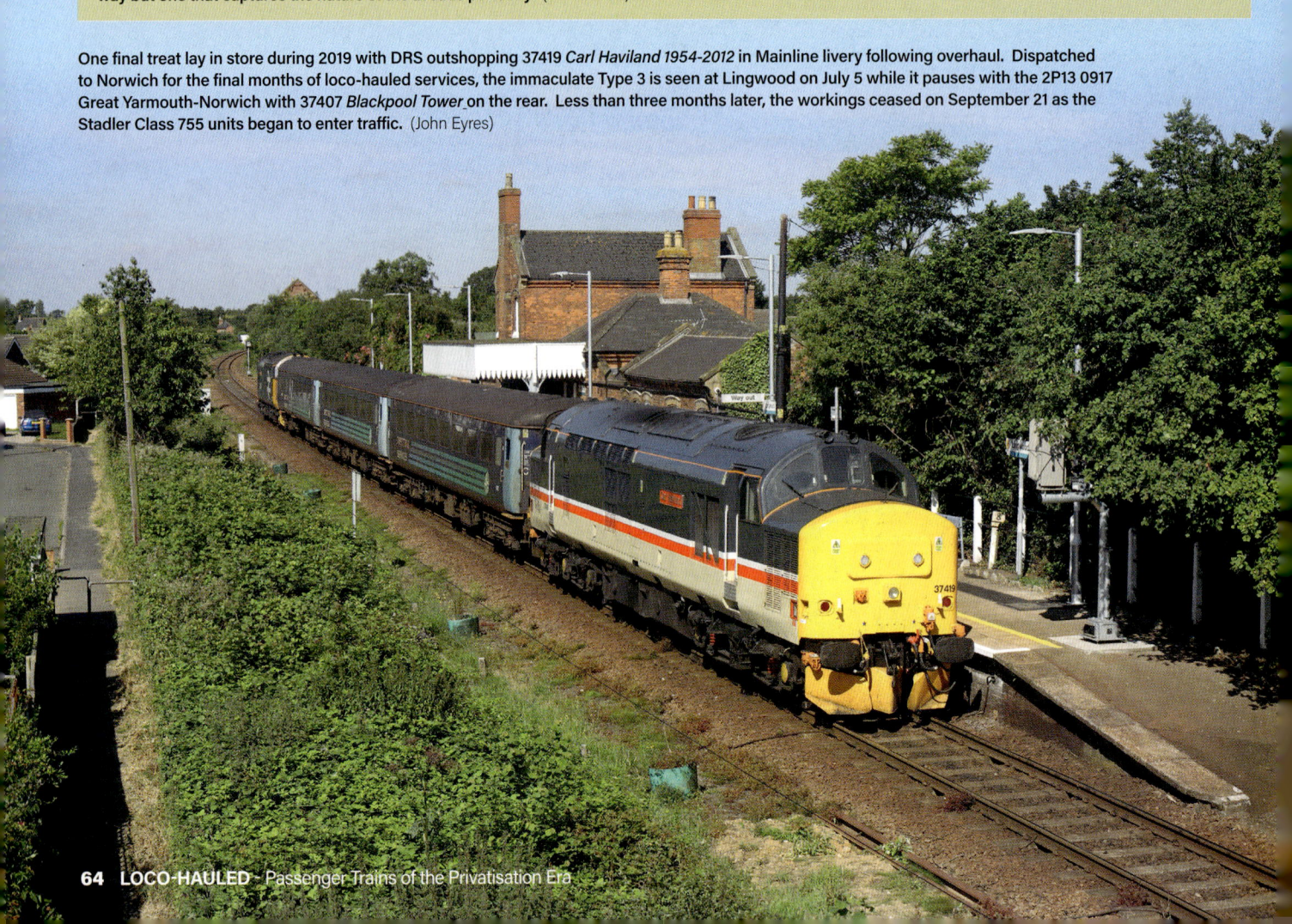

One final treat lay in store during 2019 with DRS outshopping 37419 *Carl Haviland 1954-2012* in Mainline livery following overhaul. Dispatched to Norwich for the final months of loco-hauled services, the immaculate Type 3 is seen at Lingwood on July 5 while it pauses with the 2P13 0917 Great Yarmouth-Norwich with 37407 *Blackpool Tower* on the rear. Less than three months later, the workings ceased on September 21 as the Stadler Class 755 units began to enter traffic. (John Eyres)

NEW WEBSITE LAUNCH

YOUR ONLINE HOME FOR MODERN railways

Key Modern Railways is the **NEW** online home of rail industry content, brought to you by Key Publishing, publishers of *Modern Railways* magazine.

You'll find all the latest industry news, written with authority, on Key Modern Railways - plus detailed analysis, in-depth features and website exclusives.

UNLIMITED access to this exciting online content from our dedicated team starts from just £41.99/year for UK customers. And registering couldn't be simpler. For instant access to the latest *Modern Railways* magazine features and industry-leading content, visit:

www.keymodernrailways.com

Philip Sherratt
Editor - *Modern Railways* Magazine & Key Modern Railways

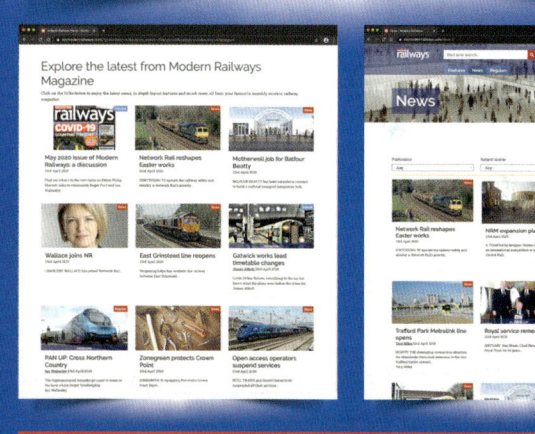

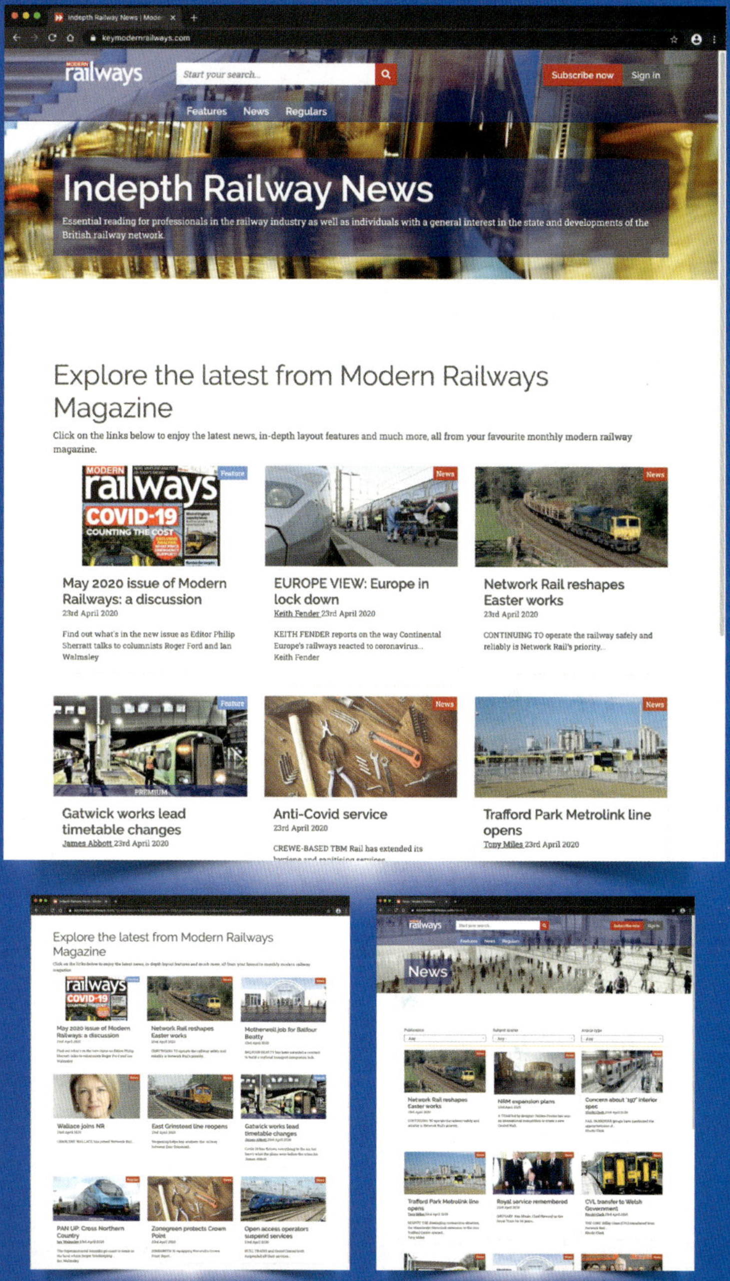

LATEST NEWS written with authority

FREE ACCESS FOR ALL MODERN railways SUBSCRIBERS*

Visit: www.keymodernrailways.com/subscribe

*Free access available for a limited time only – sign up today!

221/20

💬 **We value your feedback!** Let us know your thoughts on *Key Modern Railways* – drop us a line at subs@keypublishing.com today

ScotRail

Circling the Kingdom

December 2008 saw a Class 67-powered working commence in Scotland, this encompassing a morning and evening turn from Edinburgh Waverley to the Fife commuter belt. Introduced to allow First ScotRail DMUs to be deployed elsewhere, a second set was brought into use 12 months later for similar workings, this seeing the BR blue/grey Cargo-D Mk2s intermingle with the previously used DBS/EWS maroon Mk2s.

May 2011 saw one diagram revert to DMU operation, but this was reversed just three months later as there were still not enough units to cover all services. As a result, both Class 67-hauled sets remained in use throughout 2012 and it was not until the beginning of February 2013 that ScotRail could finally withdraw one diagram. The other continued though, largely ignored by enthusiasts, and with the DB Schenker-owned coaches becoming rapidly dilapidated, both inside and out.

By April 2014, the condition of the coaches was such that they were removed from service for much-needed attention. To provide cover, Mk2f TSOs 5945, 5952, 6067, 6176 and 6177 along with Mk2e BSO 9507 were hired from Riviera Trains, these all retaining Virgin colours. These remained in use as a stop-gap until the beginning of that July, by when the DBS Mk2s were ready to return, the repair work having included a fresh coat of maroon with gold DB logos replacing the previous EWS beasties.

A more permanent change occurred from April 1, 2015, with Abellio replacing First Group as the operator of the ScotRail franchise. The contract for the Fife Circle loco-hauled workings was awarded to Direct Rail Services, which deployed two of its then new Class 68s along with Mk2 coaches hired from Riviera Trains. Prior to the changeover, all the stock was re-liveried into the blue with white dots ScotRail livery, creating a smart and uniform appearance for the trains.

The end of 2015 saw the usefulness of the loco-hauled sets demonstrated after the Forth Road Bridge was closed to all traffic for much of December after structural issues were discovered. With extra trains laid on, the Class 68s top and tailed additional services to Fife throughout the period while the Class 67s and DB Mk2s were also brought back to provide further capacity.

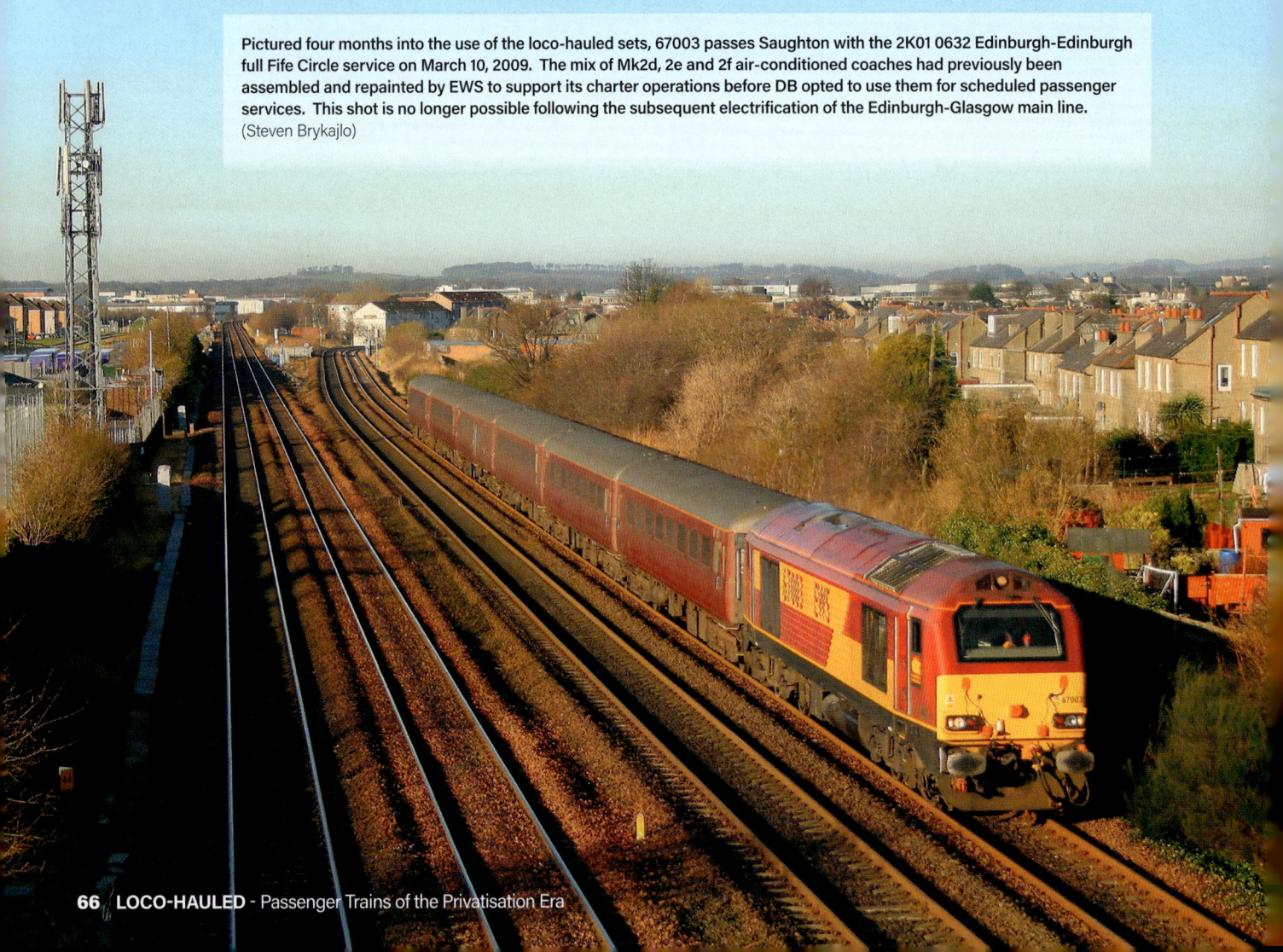

Pictured four months into the use of the loco-hauled sets, 67003 passes Saughton with the 2K01 0632 Edinburgh-Edinburgh full Fife Circle service on March 10, 2009. The mix of Mk2d, 2e and 2f air-conditioned coaches had previously been assembled and repainted by EWS to support its charter operations before DB opted to use them for scheduled passenger services. This shot is no longer possible following the subsequent electrification of the Edinburgh-Glasgow main line.
(Steven Brykajlo)

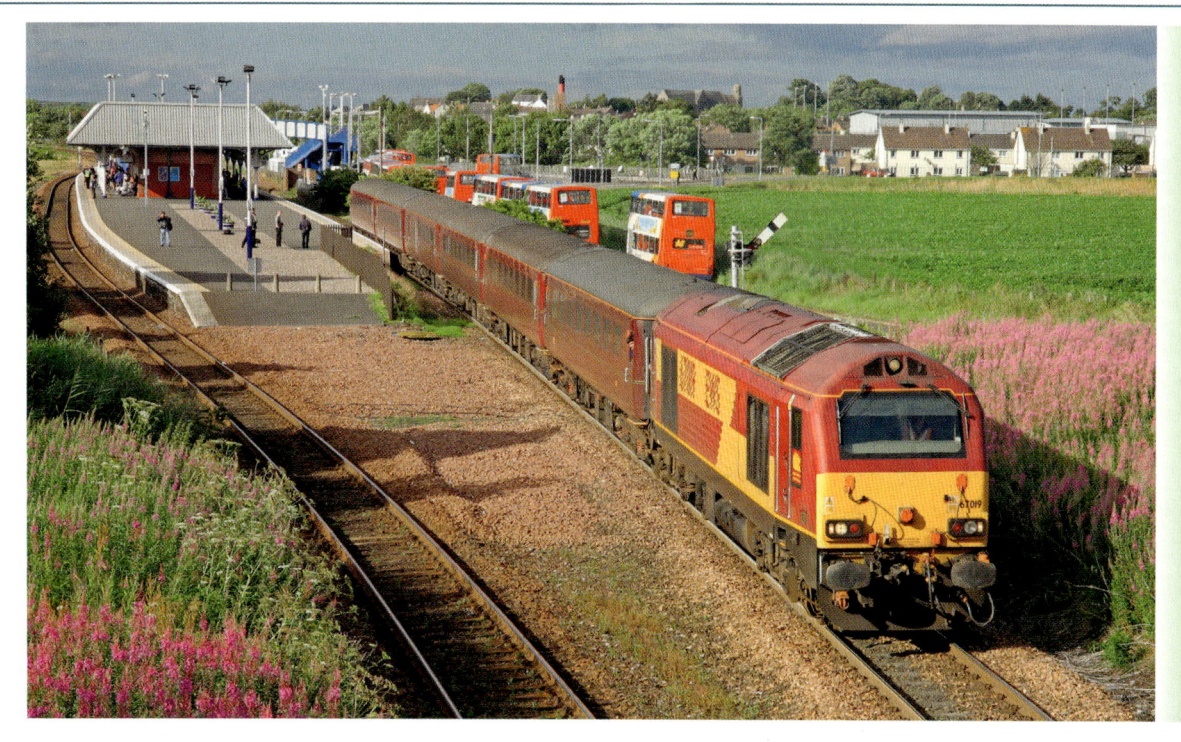

ScotRail

Under the auspices of First ScotRail, the Fife Circle sets were sometimes used to provide additional capacity during major sporting events, particularly golf tournaments at Scotland's famous courses. With the 2010 Open Championship taking place at St Andrews, 67019 is seen departing Leuchars with the 1Z16 1754 Dundee to Edinburgh working on July 16. The fleet of buses littering the station forecourt amply illustrates the need for such extra workings. (Jim Ramsay)

Finished in its unique version of the DB red livery, 67018 *Keith Heller* pauses at Haymarket on January 27, 2011, to collect weary commuters. Making up the 2G13 1708 Edinburgh-Edinburgh circular are five of the BR blue/grey Cargo-D Mk2 coaches, these appearing on the services from 2009 following the introduction of the second loco-hauled diagram. (Steven Brykajlo)

By early 2014, the DB Mk2s were in such poor condition after five years of use and minimal maintenance that they had to be removed from traffic for three months of substantial repairs and replaced by Riviera Trains stock. Returned to use that summer, the newly repainted vehicles are seen forming the 2K18 Cardenden-Edinburgh Waverley at Jamestown Viaduct on July 15. In charge was 67016, the coaches rather highlighting its own shabby condition. (Guy Houston)

LOCO-HAULED - Passenger Trains of the Privatisation Era

ScotRail

On the second and somewhat glorious morning of the new order for the Fife Circle workings, April 2, 2015, ScotRail-liveried 68006 *Daring* powers across the Forth Bridge atop the 2K18 0735 Cardenden-Edinburgh. In tow is a matching set of Mk2f coaches consisting of TSOs 5965, 5976, 6176, 6177 and 6183 along with BSO 9539, the latter being positioned in the middle of the set.
(Guy Houston)

ScotRail

ScotRail

The second ScotRail-liveried Class 68, 68007 Valiant, skirts the Firth of Forth at Burntisland on August 16, 2018, while in charge of the 2K14 1817 Glenrothes with Thornton to Edinburgh. While the two locos were nominally dedicated to the Fife Circle workings, the need for periodic maintenance and unscheduled repairs meant that one or both could be absent from the services at times with DRS-liveried sisters stepping in as cover. (Jason Cross)

Thereafter, the services operated during the morning and evening with little in the way of drama until the end of 2019 and the impending introduction of the new persons with reduced mobility (PRM) legislation. With no replacement stock available, ScotRail was granted an exemption for the Mk2s to continue in use until the end of May 2020 but the coronavirus pandemic subsequently brought the commuter services to a premature end in mid-March

However, with ScotRail still paying the hire charges for the trains until the end of May, it was decided to re-deploy both loco-hauled sets onto late evening services around the Fife Circle, these being intended for key workers with the extra length of the sets aiding social distancing measures. At the end of May, the 11 and a half years operation came to a low-key end with ScotRail subsequently abandoning any plans to bring back loco-hauled trains from December 2020 due to the reduced demand for travel.

Appropriately enough, the Fife Circle workings ended as they had begun with 68006 and 68007 in charge and during a period of good weather. By the last day, on May 29, 2020 though, the ScotRail-liveried Mk2s hired from Riviera Trains had been largely dispensed with in favour of DRS' own coaches, these having the advantage of featuring retention toilet tanks. With the previous commuter diagrams having been dropped in favour of late evening workings, 68006 Daring is seen at Auchengray with the 5K97 empty stock from Motherwell TMD to Edinburgh. This would go on to form the final ever working, the 2K97 2200 Edinburgh-Inverkeithing, and bring an end to Mk2 operation on the main line in regular passenger service. (Scott Dargavel)

70 LOCO-HAULED - Passenger Trains of the Privatisation Era

Class 90s on hire

Electrics Everywhere

As Privatisation got underway in 1996/97, the newly created EWS found itself with both the Rail Express Systems and Railfreight Distribution allocations of Class 90s. This encompassed 90016-24 and 90125-40, the latter being freight-only locos with their electric train supply isolated and notionally restricted to a maximum speed of 75mph. Freightliner was in the same position with its allocation of 90141-50 all featuring the same restrictions.

However, the brave new world of the privatised network brought opportunities to hire the locos out to any passenger companies in need of additional motive power. For EWS, this would bring the already seen openings with Virgin Cross Country, Silverlink and ScotRail in the mid 2000s while both companies would become involved with hauling the Caledonian Sleeper trains, as detailed in the next chapter.

But it was with the operators of the West Coast, East Coast and Great Eastern main lines where hire periods first presented themselves in the final years of the 20th century. As a result, both freight companies set about reversing the modifications made to their Class 90s with 90026-29 the first to regain their ETS capability and original numbers in March 1998. The remainder of 90030-40 duly followed in the summer of 1999.

In the case of Freightliner, 90142 and 90146 had both had their ability to provide ETS reinstated by early 1999 but initially they went without a change of number, this not taking place until late 2001. The remainder of the Freightliner fleet duly followed suit with both the modifications and renumbering in the late summer of 2002, albeit with the exception of 90147 which was stopped with substantial fire damage at the time and would not run again until late 2004.

As GNER and Anglia Railways passed their batons to new operators and the Virgin Trains fleet evolved, there was still a need for the freight companies' Class 90s to assist at times throughout the 2000s and even into the subsequent decade.

Between 1999 and 2002, both 90142 and 90146 spent periods on hire to Virgin Trains to supplement its own AC electric fleet, Freightliner specially reinstating the ETS equipment for this purpose. On June 16, 2000, 90146 propels an unidentified Glasgow Central-Euston service past Bessy Gill, to the south of Penrith.
(David Dockray)

LOCO-HAULED - Passenger Trains of the Privatisation Era

Class 90s on hire

EWS Class 90s were no strangers to Virgin services throughout the first half of the 2000s, be it on the longer distance workings or the shorter West Midlands diagrams that typically employed air-conditioned Mk2 stock. The evening of November 1, 2002 found SNCB-liveried 90028 *Vrachtverbinding* pausing at Birmingham International as it worked north with the 1G37 1710 Euston to Wolverhampton. Having lasted for a decade, the special Freightconnection livery would be lost six months later. (Jason Cross)

Following its involvement in the Grayrigg derailment on February 23, 2007, 'Pendolino' 390033 was written off as beyond economic repair. This decision left Virgin a unit short on an already tightly utilised fleet and forced it to return to leasing a loco-hauled set from Porterbrook. With EWS/DB providing a Class 90, the formation was kept on the West Midlands circuits as much as possible. On September 4 the same year, 90034 hurries the 1G21 1651 Euston-Birmingham New Street through Chelmscote, to the north of Leighton Buzzard. (Bill Atkinson)

Somewhat reluctantly, Virgin had to retain the services of this single Mk3 set, it duly spending over half of 2009 undergoing refurbishment. To provide cover during its absence, a scratch set of sister vehicles was hired from Cargo-D, this featuring a messy mix of Virgin and BR blue/grey liveries. Initially intended for relief use only, a collision between two 'Pendolinos' at Wembley that March saw it placed in daily use between London and Birmingham. On April 20, 2009, the set is seen near Blisworth while heading for New Street on the 1G30 1543 departure from Euston. In charge was 90036, this still retaining the experimental version of the Railfreight Distribution European livery applied way back in October 1992. By now somewhat weather beaten, the 'subtle' EWS beasties logo was added in June 2006. (Nigel Gibbs)

Class 90s on hire

When the refurnished Mk3 set was released from Wabtec, Doncaster, in July 2009, it soon gained the nickname of the 'Pretendolino' as it carried the same silver and red livery as the Class 390s. Officially known by its set number of WB64, this denoting its allocation to Wembley, the formation featured five TSO, a buffet, three FO and the strikingly finished DVT 82126. Initially, traction continued to be supplied by DB Schenker with any of its colourful Class 90 fleet capable of appearing. On April 23, 2010, it was the turn of First ScotRail-liveried 90021 to take charge as it speeds though Gayton, near Northampton, with the 1G27 1443 Euston-Birmingham New Street. (Matthew Clarke)

For the second half of 2010, the Mk3 set had only one regular working, a Fridays-only relief from Euston to Preston, although it did appear as and when required on other diagrams as well as charters, such as specials for football supporters. A significant change from December 23 that year saw Freightliner replace DB as the supplier of the Class 90, as seen a month later on January 31, 2011, as 90047 leads the 1G27 1443 Euston-Birmingham New Street through Chelmscote. The first two months of the year saw the 'Pretendolino' deployed regularly on Birmingham workings. (Andrew Chambers)

LOCO-HAULED - Passenger Trains of the Privatisation Era

Class 90s on hire

Repainted the previous summer, 90045 was still looking smart in the 'PowerHaul' version of the Freightliner livery at it hurried through Tile Hill on February 24, 2011, with the 1G15 1043 Euston-New Street. The diagram at this time covered three round trips between London and Birmingham before a one-way working to Crewe in the evening and an empty stock return to the capital. Over the course of Freightliner's tenure, all of the company's Class 90 fleet appeared on the set in the form of 90016 and 90041-49. (Matthew Clarke).

By the beginning of 2014, the use of the Mk3 set had become rather limited but, with increasing passenger numbers, it was brought back into use to form additional services on Thursday and Friday evenings. Given it had no electric locos at the time, Direct Rail Services was surprisingly awarded the haulage contract, it duly reaching agreement with DB Schenker to hire a single Class 90. The selected machine, 90034, was repainted into DRS colours with the set returning to use from the start of April on Euston-Birmingham workings. Although a two-year contract had been agreed, this was terminated just six months later as part of the conditions surrounding the granting of a franchise extension to Virgin. On June 6 that year, 90034 is seen at Ledburn Junction heading a delayed 1G40 1903 Euston-Birmingham. (Andrew Chambers)

Class 90s on hire

Between 1998 and 2002, GNER hired a single Class 90 from EWS to first supplement its fleet of Class 91s and then provide cover for them while they underwent a substantial life-extension overhaul programme. Generally, the hire-in was placed on a King's Cross to Leeds/Bradford diagram and this was the case on May 22, 1999, as another of the Freightconnection trio, 90029 *Frachtverbindungen*, heads the 1D40 1430 departure to Leeds at Broad Fen Lane, Claypole. The loco would swap its DB livery for EWS maroon in April 2003. (Bill Atkinson)

While the refurbishment of the Class 91s was ongoing, Freightliner also provided assistance at times. On September 10, 2001, 90142 departs from Doncaster at the rear of a GNER Leeds service bound for King's Cross. Between 2000 and 2002, this Class 90 amassed thousands of passenger miles working for Virgin, GNER and Anglia Railways. (John Turner)

After a barren few years on the East Coast Main Line, Class 90s returned in October 2016, this time on hire to Virgin Trains. Initially, one DB example was brought in to help ease the burden on the hard-pressed Class 91s and allow a backlog of maintenance work to be undertaken with a second arriving from the early summer of 2017. This arrangement continued even after the franchise was brought back under government control as LNER in June 2018 and on April 20 the following year, 90029 is seen approaching Sandy with the 1D22 1633 King's Cross-Leeds. However, just under two months later, the hire was brought to an end as the first Class 800 'Azumas' were introduced. (Nigel Gibbs)

LOCO-HAULED - Passenger Trains of the Privatisation Era

Class 90s on hire

Much like Virgin and GNER, Anglia Railways also called in Class 90s to bolster its fleet at times of poor availability. In Anglia's case, this was most evident in 2002/03 as the Class 86s began to show their age and the franchise drew to a close. On March 22, 2003, 90050 lays over at Norwich as it awaits departure back to London with the 1430 service to Liverpool Street. The last of the fleet was only 18 months away from suffering severe and ultimately terminal fire damage, the heavily stripped shell still awaiting disposal in 2020. (Gareth Bayer)

When National Express took over the Anglia franchise under the 'One' brand in April 2004, it turned to EWS for assistance as the fleet transitioned from Class 86, Mk2 and DBSO formations to Class 90s, Mk3s and DVTs displaced from the West Coast Main Line. If this was not difficult enough, the new arrivals also had to be cycled through refurbishment and repainting programmes with staff training also taking place. Having a few extra locos on hand was a sensible move as evidenced on June 8 that year as Rail Express Systems-liveried 90019 *Penny Black* leaves Norwich behind as it passes Trowse with the 1140 service to London. (Gareth Bayer)

76 LOCO-HAULED - Passenger Trains of the Privatisation Era

Class 90s on hire

Another example of an EWS machine on hire to National Express, 90021 displays its Railfreight Distribution European livery as it heads the 1500 Norwich-Liverpool Street 'One' service. The fully extended pantograph gives a clue that the train is approaching a level crossing, in this case at Newton Flotman, with the date being May 10, 2004.
(Gareth Bayer)

Moving on to 2008 and hired in Class 90s could still be seen working alongside their leased sisters with National Express East Anglia. In charge of the 1P37 1300 Norwich-Liverpool Street, 90021 was far away from the operator whose livery it now carried for sleeper services as it passes Kelvedon, between Colchester and Chelmsford, on April 10, 2008. (Bill Atkinson)

Following the demise of the 'Pretendolino' with Virgin Trains in October 2014, the stock was duly hired by Greater Anglia for two years to bolster its own Mk3 fleet. On August 3, 2015, the set found itself reunited with 90034, the loco also being on long term hire to the company. Still retaining DRS blue but with the logos removed in favour of DB cabside badges, the formation is seen at Dunston forming the 1P57 1730 Norwich to Liverpool Street.
(Jamie Squibbs)

LOCO-HAULED - Passenger Trains of the Privatisation Era

Scottish Sleepers

Through the Night

With the preparation of the various passenger units for privatisation, the Anglo-Scottish sleeper operation was transferred from InterCity West Coast to ScotRail in March 1995. At this time, the future of the service was mired in politics with British Rail making strenuous efforts to withdraw the Fort William portion, only to lose a legal challenge brought by the Highland Regional Council and eventually abandon its plan.

Rebranded as the Caledonian Sleeper, all the services, including those to London, were included in the ScotRail franchise that was awarded to National Express, this commencing at the end of March 1997. One consequence of the removal of the sleepers from the West Coast portfolio was the need to arrange a new hire agreement to continue to use AC electrics from what was now the Virgin Trains fleet to power the overnight legs from Euston to Edinburgh and Glasgow. This arrangement only lasted for a further 12 months before EWS stepped in with Class 90s. The freight company had already inherited responsibility for powering the diesel portions when it took control of Rail Express Systems in December 1995 and Transrail two months later, with Class 47s in use on the Inverness and Aberdeen portions and a Class 37/4 working to Fort William.

By the end of the decade, the refurbishment and upgrading of the sleeper stock was underway, this seeing the provision of converted Mk2e Brake Unclassified Open (BUO) coaches to allow seated passengers to be conveyed once again while the Caledonian Sleeper brand appeared externally as part of a new two-tone purple livery. Developments on the motive power front saw Class 67s begin to appear between Edinburgh and Inverness/Aberdeen from September 2000 with ScotRail wanting rid of the Class 47s; a more permanent exchange occurring two years later.

From October 17, 2004, First Group took over the ScotRail franchise, it largely maintaining the status quo in terms of locos and stock. The exception was the West Highland Line where both First and EWS wanted a Class 67 to

Looking more like 1995 than 1999, the National Express brand had yet to reach the West Highland sleeper on July 28 as 37410 *Aluminium 100* powers through the early morning sunlight at Bridge of Orchy with the 1Y11 0450 Edinburgh-Fort William. Given the amount of exhaust emanating from the Type 3, hopefully the sleeper passengers were enjoying their 12 cylinder alarm call! (Phil Chilton)

78 LOCO-HAULED - Passenger Trains of the Privatisation Era

Scottish Sleepers

Over on the other sleeper routes, Rail Express Systems Class 47s still dominated proceedings initially as shown on May 13, 1998, as 47760 *Restless* powers through a moody Crubenmore, to the north of Dalwhinnie, with the morning portion to Inverness. The nine-coach formation is made up of seven Mk3a sleepers, a Mk2f Lounge car and a Mk1 Full Brake. (David Dockray)

replace the Class 37/4, Network Rail objecting due to the axle weight of the GMs being far in excess of what was normally permitted. It was not until June 2006 that the switchover was finally permitted but with a lengthy list of speed restrictions imposed on the Class 67s to reduce the impact on the numerous bridges.

Major changes came to the Caledonian Sleepers from March 31, 2015, with Serco taking charge of the now independent operation, having been split from ScotRail as part of the latest round of franchise re-tendering. With Serco having appointed GB Railfreight as its traction provider, the intention was to use overhauled Class 92s on the WCML services with re-engineered Class 73/9s taking over the Scottish portions, all of which would eventually be formed of new CAF-built Mk5 stock to replace the existing Mk2/3 sets.

Initially, the Class 92s worked alongside DB Class 90s, the intention being to fully transition over to the Brush electrics as more were refurbished. However, numerous reliability problems soon became apparent with the '92s', caused in part by fluctuating voltages from the 25kV electrification that upset their sensitive electronics. With the locos largely removed from traffic while investigations and then modifications were undertaken, DB Class 90s first provided cover, working with the trio of 86101, 86401 and 87002, which were upgraded from their initial role of undertaking empty stock moves. From August 2015, Freightliner Class 90s were hired in as a more long term solution, this mix of motive power continuing but gradually reducing throughout 2016-18 as the Class 92s returned and settled down. Even then, it took the introduction of the Mk5s during 2019 to finally see off the Freightliner '90s', these

Two months before the sleepers passed into private hands, 87020 *North Briton* makes its booked stop at Crewe just before midnight on January 9, 1997. Heading the 1S25 2130 Euston-Inverness, the AC electric would also become a Virgin loco from March 1997, the company only providing sleeper traction for another year thereafter. (Neil Harvey)

LOCO-HAULED - Passenger Trains of the Privatisation Era   79

Scottish Sleepers

Due to weight restrictions on the West Highland Line, the EWS Class 37/4s remained in charge of the sleeper portions on the route throughout the tenure of National Express. Not that enthusiasts were complaining when there were sights like this to enjoy as 37421 slogs along near the summit of County March with the 1Y11 Edinburgh-Fort William. Formed of a short rake of refurbished stock, the date was May 4, 2002. *(Jimmy Wilson)*

During 2002, EWS and ScotRail signed a new haulage contract for the sleepers, this specifying that only Class 67s should be used on the Inverness and Aberdeen legs as the passenger operator had become tired of the foibles of the Class 47s. Apart from a few odd Type 4 appearances during the year, this was largely achieved. During May 2002, the new order of General Motors power is seen near Tomatin as 67028 heads for the Highland capital with the 1S25 working from Euston. *(Bob Avery)*

being incompatible with the new coaches, with the Class 92s left to go it alone thereafter.

In Scotland, the Class 67s were initially retained upon Serco's takeover in the spring of 2015 ahead of a protracted switch to the Class 73/9s with the new order attempting a full takeover in July 2016. This proved to be premature as the electro-diesels were far from reliable, the new alternator sets being particularly prone to vibration issues. Again, investigations and alterations were put in hand while the Scottish sleeper portions were largely kept running using Class 66 and Class 73/9 combinations, the latter being solely used as a source of electrical power for the train.

A Class 67 was also retained on hire and deployed as necessary, this becoming a regular feature on the Inverness sleeper from the spring of 2017. This allowed the pressure to be eased on the Class 73/9s while 73969 received lengthy repairs to collision damage sustained in a shunting incident. In addition, Dellner couplings needed to be fitted to the former Southern locos and testing undertaken with the Mk5s. The new stock was introduced to passenger service on all three routes in October 2019, this bringing the end of the Class 67 on the Inverness portion. Since then, the Class 73/9s have largely managed on their own, although at times the Inverness 'beds' have seen a single Class 73 receive assistance from a Class 66, either due to low availability or, as during the spring 2020 lockdown, to ensure no reliability problems on the journey.

LOCO-HAULED - Passenger Trains of the Privatisation Era

Scottish Sleepers

For the West Coast legs, EWS Class 90s held total control at this time, only really attracting attention when some overnight incident had caused delays. Such was the case on October 27, 2004, when 90019 *Penny Black* was recorded hurrying north through Docker, Cumbria, at 0948 with the previous night's Euston to Edinburgh and Glasgow train, this running some five hours late! Just 10 days earlier, the ScotRail franchise and thus the sleepers had passed to First Group control. (David Dockray)

Apart from the First logos adorning three of the coaches, the new operator of the Caledonian Sleeper was in no hurry to stamp its identity on the service when the Fort William 'beds' were recorded crossing Rannoch Viaduct on March 4, 2005. With the cold and frost only serving to further highlight the majesty of the area, the electric train supply of 37406 *The Saltire Society* was keeping the passengers warm on the 1Y11 0450 from Edinburgh. (Scott Borthwick)

LOCO-HAULED - Passenger Trains of the Privatisation Era   81

Scottish Sleepers

Having clung on for far longer than expected, the use of a Class 37/4 on the Fort William sleeper finally came to an end on June 9, 2006, after the Class 67s gained approval to work on the West Highland. A month earlier, on May 10, 37406 *The Saltire Society* was preparing for the end as it once again took 1Y11 north past the popular photographic location of Achallader, to the north of Bridge of Orchy. By this time, the application of First Group colours to the coaches was underway with the RFO and BUO both repainted in blue but awaiting the application of the white and magenta stripes. (Bill Atkinson)

As part of EWS' traction agreement with First Group, three Class 90s were repainted in the latter's colours in order to match the re-liveried sleeper stock. While 90019 and 90024 were both completed in the summer of 2006, 90021 did not follow until the start of 2007. As usual, little attempt was made to dedicate the locos to the sleepers, the trio working freely on both freight and other passenger duties. However, on December 28, 2013, a grubby 90024 was in the right place atop the 1M16 2044 Inverness-Euston as it passes Chelmscote. It was definitely not the right time though with the sleeper running over four hours late. (Nigel Gibbs)

82 LOCO-HAULED - Passenger Trains of the Privatisation Era

Scottish Sleepers

An early morning lineside visit to Old Linslade, Leighton Buzzard, on July 6, 2013, was rewarded with the sight of newly repainted 90036 heading for the capital at 0705. The sparkling electric had taken over the 1M16 working at Edinburgh around 0100 that morning, this featuring the portions from Fort William,. Inverness and Aberdeen combined into one train for the onward trip to Euston. (Nigel Gibbs)

In order for the Class 67s to work on the West Highland, five examples (67004/07/09/11/30) were fitted with RETB radio signalling equipment while all bar 67030 also received harder-wearing cast iron brake blocks in 2007 to cope with the number of speed restrictions that had to be braked for. Once the brake wear problem had been solved, the class went on to cope well enough with the demands of the line even if they were never an ideal choice. On July 21, 2014, 67009 stands in the shadow of Ben Nevis as it passes Torlundy on the approach to Fort William. (Mark Fielding)

LOCO-HAULED - Passenger Trains of the Privatisation Era

Scottish Sleepers

Looking smart in the midnight teal livery adopted for the independent Caledonian Sleeper operation, overhauled 92038 hums through Harringay on the diverted 1M16 2044 Inverness-Euston on April 7, 2015, this being the first week of Serco's tenure. Over the past five years, considerable use has been made of the East Coast Main Line as a diversionary route during engineering work or unplanned disruption, King's Cross even serving as the London terminus on a handful of occasions. (Nigel Gibbs)

To undertake empty stock movements between Euston and Wembley along with Glasgow Central and Polmadie, GB Railfreight hired 86101, 86401 and 87002 from Electric Traction Ltd, all being duly repainted. At the time, no one could have predicted just how vital they would become to keeping the sleepers running as the Class 92 reliability problems surfaced. Of the three, 87002 *Royal Sovereign* shouldered a lot of work and is seen coasting through Harrow & Wealdstone on April 28, 2015, with the 1M16 2044 Inverness-Euston. (Nigel Gibbs)

The bulk of the Class 92 covering was done by the Freightliner Class 90s, these arriving from August 2015 and remaining until October 2019, although the greatest use was during the first half of this period when up to three examples could be needed per night. On April 25, 2017, 90043 powers through Ashton, to the north of Milton Keynes, as it seeks to make up over an hour's delay to 1M16 caused by overhead line damage around Lancaster. (Nigel Gibbs)

84 LOCO-HAULED - Passenger Trains of the Privatisation Era

Scottish Sleepers

For the launch of Serco's tenure in March 2015, DB repainted 67004 into the midnight teal livery, the loco also gaining the name *Cairn Gorm* the same month. Four weeks later, the loco was recorded slumbering at Fort William on May 2 ahead of working back to Edinburgh that evening with the 1B01 departure. (Guy Houston)

On three weekends in February 2016, the Fort William sleeper was diverted to Oban due to engineering work, this bringing some of the first passenger workings for the Class 73/9s as the hired-in Class 67 was not permitted over the weight restricted line. On the last of these occasions, February 27, 73968 and 73967 had earlier top and tailed the 1Y11 0450 Edinburgh to Oban and are pictured crossing the end of Loch Awe with the returning 5Y11 1030 Oban-Polmadie empty stock. With no servicing facilities for the coaches at their altered destination, the train had to run back to Glasgow to be attended to and then return to Oban the following day for that night's service to London. The ex Virgin RFO and InterCity BSO were amongst a handful of Riviera Trains Mk2f coaches then on hire to Serco to provide additional 'day' coaches. (Jim Ramsay)

LOCO-HAULED - Passenger Trains of the Privatisation Era   85

Scottish Sleepers

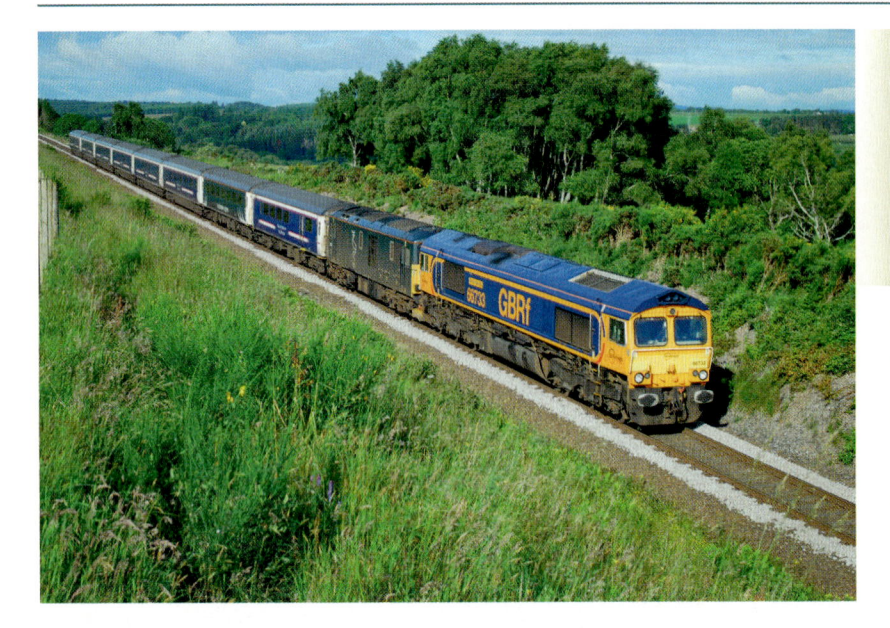

When the alternator problems struck the Class 73/9s, they were largely reduced to the role of mobile train supply units as this would not place a strain on the power unit. Instead, a GBRf Class 66 was provided to haul the train with the electro-diesel coupled behind. On July 13, 2016, it was the turn of 66733 *Cambridge PSB* and 73967 to team up to get the 1S25 0415 Edinburgh-Inverness to its destination, the duo being recorded at Culloden. (Roddy MacPhee)

Throughout the struggles with Class 73/9 availability, some measure of assistance was provided by Class 47s, although with their own tendency to misbehave, they were only used when necessary. Such was the case on May 19, 2018, when 47727 was entrusted with the 1A25 0443 Edinburgh-Aberdeen, it being recorded approaching Arbroath at the site of the former Elliot Junction. This was the Type 4's first time out in the Caledonian Sleeper teal livery and it had yet to receive its stag brandings or *Edinburgh Castle/Caisteal Dhùn Èideann* nameplates. (Jim Ramsay)

The Mk5 stock was finally introduced to the Highland sleepers from October 2019 after a troubled testing and commissioning process. From this date, only Class 73/9s have been used on the Fort William and Aberdeen portions, the use of Dellner couplings preventing anything else from appearing. On January 18, 2020, 73971 had worked the 1A25 0439 Edinburgh-Aberdeen and was now taking the empty stock back to Polmadie ahead of an engineering blockade. With the local populace taking no notice, the 5Z25 working is seen passing Arbroath Golf Course while the next evening would see the sleeper start from Dundee. (Jim Ramsay)

86 LOCO-HAULED - Passenger Trains of the Privatisation Era

Scottish Sleepers

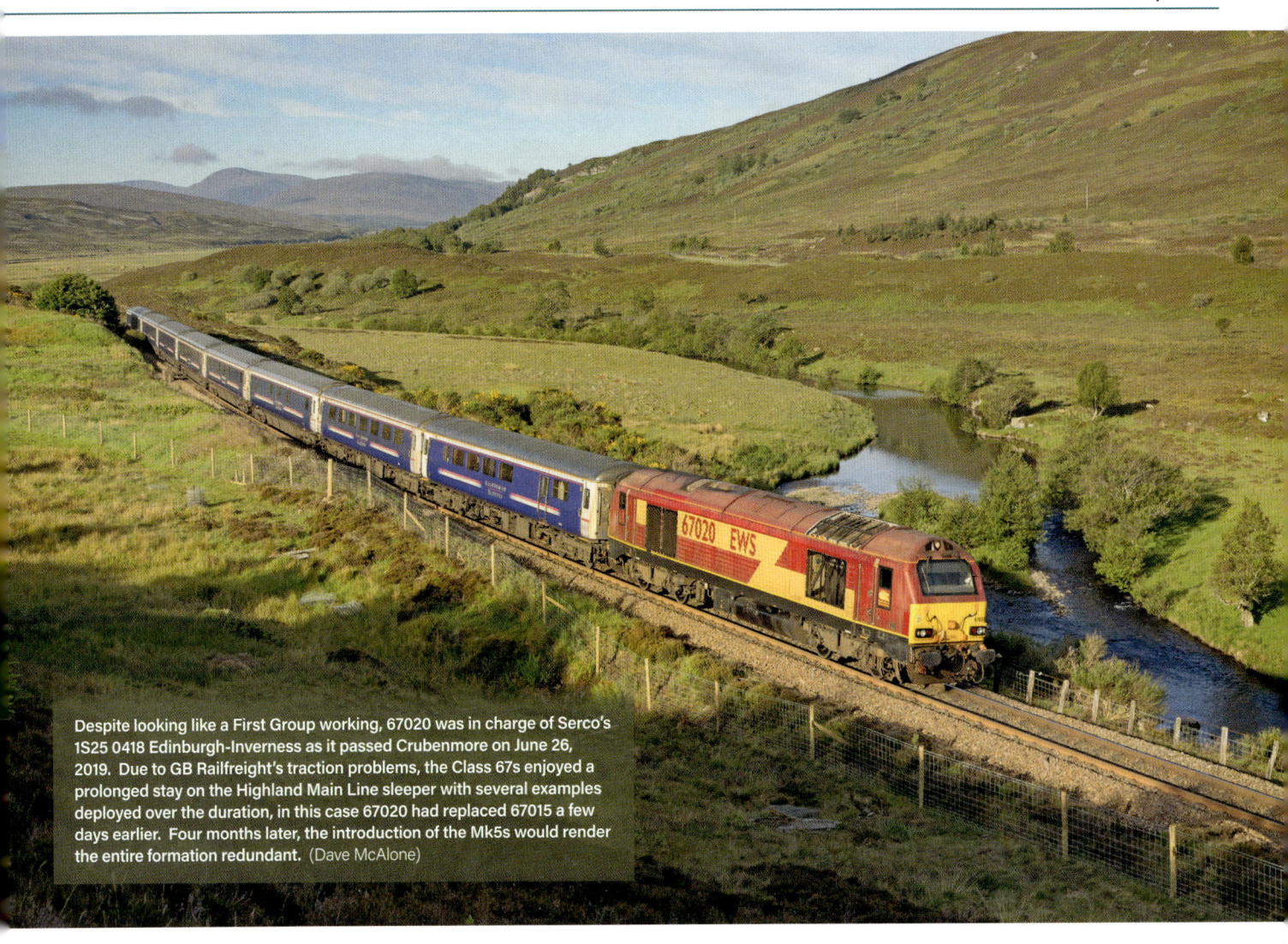

Despite looking like a First Group working, 67020 was in charge of Serco's 1S25 0418 Edinburgh-Inverness as it passed Crubenmore on June 26, 2019. Due to GB Railfreight's traction problems, the Class 67s enjoyed a prolonged stay on the Highland Main Line sleeper with several examples deployed over the duration, in this case 67020 had replaced 67015 a few days earlier. Four months later, the introduction of the Mk5s would render the entire formation redundant. (Dave McAlone)

With the transition from old to new completed, the look of the Caledonian Sleeper for years to come is exhibited by 92018 on June 25, 2020, as it brings a full 16-coach Mk5 formation south at Mancetter, near Nuneaton. Due to the Covid-19 pandemic and reduced services as a result, this was running as the amended and combined 1M16 2045 Inverness/Glasgow to Euston. (Jason Cross)

LOCO-HAULED - Passenger Trains of the Privatisation Era

SUBSCRIBE TODAY
SAVE UP TO 45%

Enjoy the latest news and features anytime, anywhere!

BEST VALUE

	Print	Digital	Print + Digital
Printed magazine	✓	✗	✓
Digital edition	✗	✓	✓
No delivery charges	✓	✓	✓
Exclusive subscriber discounts	✓	✓	✓
	from **£40.99***	**£34.99**	from **£55.99***
	Save up to 30%	Instant access	Save up to 45%

Gifts available with Print+Digital and Print subscriptions

For our full range of subscription terms and offers visit our website

* Quoted subscription rates are for UK subscriptions paying by Direct Debit.

Direct Debit · MasterCard · PayPal · VISA

PRINT
THE CLASSIC OPTION
Each issue of your favourite magazine delivered FREE to your door.

DIGITAL
THE CONVENIENT OPTION
Instant access to every new issue, wherever you are in the world.

PRINT + DIGITAL
THE BEST VALUE OPTION
The best of both worlds - print and instant access combined.

VISIT: shop.keypublishing.com/mrsubs

USA customer? VISIT www.imsnews.com/mr **or CALL** toll-free 757-428-8180

Your customer code is: TRAVELSP20

Offer closes: 30 November 2020

Enjoy Modern railways wherever you are in the world

- **No need to wait for delivery**
- **Instant access**
- **Never miss an issue**
- **Guaranteed the best deal when you buy direct**

International Customer? Visit our website for latest subscription offers.

Modern railways

Subscribers get free access to Key Modern Railways – your new online home for rail industry news and analysis

www.keymodernrailways.com/subscribe

CALL US NOW: +44(0) 1780 480404

Lines open Monday to Friday 9.00am until 5.30pm **GMT**

Print, digital and bundle subscriptions: Quoted subscription rates are for UK subscriptions paying by Direct Debit. Quoted savings are based on UK Direct Debit rates versus purchase of individual print and digital products. Subscription gifts where offered subject to availability and subscription term. If advertised gift is not available, an alternative gift of equal value will be offered. Standard 1-year print subscription prices: UK - £50.99, EU - £61.99, USA - £57.50, ROW - £64.99.

Wrexham/Chiltern

Wrexham Wranglings

The autumn of 2007 saw the Office of Rail Regulation give approval for the commencement of an open access passenger service by the newly created Wrexham, Shropshire & Marylebone Railway. These services were designed to improve connections between the Welsh borders area and London but, with no DMUs available, the trains would be formed of a Class 67 working in push-pull mode with a Mk3b DVT and ex Virgin Mk3 coaches.

All of the Mk3 passenger stock first required extensive refurbishment while the selected DB-owned locos of 67012-15, later to be joined by 67010, needed to be fitted with remote fire extinguisher equipment so they could be left unmanned when propelling. Thus, when driver training commenced in February 2008, it was with a mix of top and tail classmates along with 67029 and DB management train DVT 82146, all paired with Cargo-D Mk3s.

As planned, passenger services commenced two months later, albeit with Wrexham & Shropshire and EWS-liveried GMs operating in top and tail mode due to the over-running refurbishment of the Mk3 stock. Also, in subsequent months Royal claret-liveried 67006 and silver 67029 were noted on the trains but deliveries of the overhauled DVTs commenced in the autumn of 2008, allowing the workings to progressively switch to push-pull format and largely with the intended fleet of Class 67s.

While the operation was well regarded by passengers, Wrexham & Shropshire struggled to make a profit amid a severe recession and was hampered by the very late delivery of the upgraded coaches. Sub-optimal timetabling was also an issue, as this affected journey times compared to rival franchised operators.

Having become wholly owned by DB Regio in 2009, the plug was pulled on Wrexham & Shropshire with very little notice on January 28, 2011. This was not without controversy though as the company was showing signs of recovery while the near immediate transfer of the loco-hauled sets to subsidiary Chiltern Railways also raised questions, especially as the latter had been planning to enhance its services between London and Birmingham for some time but was short of the necessary quality rolling stock to carry this out.

The de-branded Mk3s were deployed onto Birmingham services from the May 2011 timetable change, with the Class 67s remaining fully in charge until December 2014. From this date, a phased changeover to DRS-owned Class 68s began, the two related loco designs running alongside each other until May 27, 2015, when 67014 was released by Chiltern. As well as silver/grey 68010-015, Chiltern was given the use of the DRS-liveried pair of 68008 and 68009 as required. Nominally spare locos, they are nowadays employed just as regularly as their sisters.

The launch of the Wrexham & Shropshire services did not go as smoothly as intended as none of the refurbished Mk3s were ready nor were the overhauled and modified DVTs. As a result, BR blue/grey Mk3s had to be hired in from Cargo-D and top and tail Class 67s employed. While it got the operation off the ground, it gave the impression of a company that was not quite ready. On the first day of the open access services, April 28, 2008, 67013 and 67015 head south at Claydon Crossing with the 1P03 0725 Wrexham General-London Marylebone. Also in use on this day were 67012/14 and 67025/26 on two other Mk3 sets with 67017 becoming involved later in the day after loco problems. (Scott Borthwick)

Wrexham/Chiltern

The need to top and tail services continued well into the autumn of 2008, reducing in turn as each DVT was delivered. On September 20 that year, the EWS-liveried duo of 67017 *Arrow* and 67003 climb Hatton Bank while in charge of the 1J86 1217 Marylebone to Wrexham General. By this date, some of the Mk3s had received Wrexham & Shropshire logos to at least give the trains some sort of identity. (Scott Bortwick)

By early 2009, four DVTs were available allowing all of the Wrexham & Shropshire services to operate in push-pull format as the vehicles had been modified to work with the AAR multiple working system of the Class 67s. However, there was still no sign of the correct coaches with Cargo-D and additional DB Regio-owned Mk3s continuing to substitute. On September 9 that year, 67013 *Dyfrbont Pontcysyllte* brings the 1P03 0723 Wrexham General-Marylebone into Banbury and past the popular photographic spot alongside the Lafarge aggregates terminal. (Scott Borthwick)

LOCO-HAULED - Passenger Trains of the Privatisation Era 91

Wrexham/Chiltern

The first of the refurbished and silver-liveried Mk3s finally arrived in September 2009, with the rest trickling through over the next six months, thus allowing Wrexham & Shropshire to form up its trains as intended at long last. On March 7, 2010, 67012 *A Shropshire Lad* is seen propelling northwards at Tile Hill with the 1J41 0834 Marylebone to Wrexham General.
(Jason Cross)

Viewed from the DVT end for a change, 82305 leads an overhauled set past Ardley Quarry on October 7, 2010, this forming the 1P13 1127 Wrexham General to Marylebone. Propelling from the rear is the unmistakably-liveried 67018 *Keith Heller* in its Canadian maple leaf-branded DB red livery. Although five silver/grey Class 67s were available for the services, other examples could still appear as long as they had received the remote fire extinguishers and other modifications, 67018 being a frequent performer.
(Martin Loader)

Perhaps foreshadowing what was to come, 82302 was the final DVT to appear from overhaul in September 2009, the best part of a year after its stablemates. This was surprisingly finished in a new version of the Chiltern Railways blue and white livery but otherwise still employed between Wrexham and Marylebone. Typically, it was paired with the remaining unrefurbished Mk3s in a mix of blue/grey and de-branded Virgin colours rather than the silver sets. Following the axing of Wrexham and Shropshire, this colourful set also moved to Chiltern control and was regularly deployed on the Marylebone to Banbury commuter diagram. On June 3, 2011, the DVT leads the 1U53 1816 service to Banbury as 67013 provides power from the rear at Kings Sutton. (Martin Loader)

92 LOCO-HAULED - Passenger Trains of the Privatisation Era

Wrexham/Chiltern

The previously mentioned 67018 *Keith Heller* is seen more clearly on July 14, 2011, as it thunders through Hatton with the 1H33 1055 Birmingham Moor Street-Marylebone. This was some two months after the loco-hauled sets had been introduced on Chiltern Railways diagrams to Birmingham with the coaches stripped of their previous Wrexham & Shropshire logos. (Scott Borthwick)

Under Chiltern, the loco-hauled services came to be branded as Mainline with much effort expended on marketing the benefits of the 'silver trains' to business travellers. The existing livery was subtly tweaked with the addition of blue stripes and Chiltern logos, although the locos were left unbranded. On December 15, 2012, a driverless 67013 *Dyfrbont Pontcysyllte* passes Bordesley Junction as it nears its destination of Birmingham Moor Street with the 1R25 1106 departure from London, this being the first weekend use of the loco-hauled sets. The preceding months had seen all the silver Mk3s undergo further modernisation, including the fitting of swing-plug powered doors, thereby making them compliant with the 2020 accessibility legislation, albeit after a few minor adjustments in 2019. (Phil Chilton)

LOCO-HAULED - Passenger Trains of the Privatisation Era

Wrexham/Chiltern

Some of Chiltern's loco-hauled services extend beyond Moor Street to include other destinations around the Birmingham conurbation. On August 26, 2016, 68015 blasts out of Hampstead Tunnel as it gets into its stride with the 1K45 1615 Marylebone to Kidderminster. Of all the silver and grey Class 68s, 68015 is the only one to carry Chiltern Railways branding, this having been applied earlier that year prior to visiting a diesel gala at the Severn Valley Railway. (Tim Easter)

One of the DRS 'spares', 68008 *Avenger* takes the climb up Hatton bank in its stride as it leads the 1G40 1336 London Marylebone-Birmingham Snow Hill on April 6, 2015. Along with 68009, the loco has seen regular use with Chiltern, so much so that it is fairly unusual to see the pair on other work for any length of time. (Scott Borthwick)

94 LOCO-HAULED - Passenger Trains of the Privatisation Era

Wrexham/Chiltern

Marylebone is now the only London terminus to play host to diesel-hauled passenger trains within working hours. During the early evening of August 3, 2017, 68015 waits to depart with the 1K50 1715 Mainline service to Kidderminster while 68008 would follow it with the 1U50 1721 to Bicester North. The latter is formed of the slam-door Banbury commuter set, by then repainted in a silver and white version of the Chiltern livery to differentiate it. This set was withdrawn in the spring of 2020 as its accessibility legislation exemption ran out. Completing the line-up was 168218. (Simon McComb)

Chiltern Railways has no immediate plans to replace its loco-hauled sets with the modernised Mk3s being fit for a good few years yet. It is also one of the few routes on which such workings can now be sampled, albeit in a rather sanitised form due to the lack of opening windows. On March 28, 2019, 68015 is seen at Hatton North Junction in charge of the 1R33 1310 London Marylebone-Birmingham Moor Street. (Mark Few)

LOCO-HAULED - Passenger Trains of the Privatisation Era   95

Northern Rail

The Call of the North

The Northern Rail franchise under the joint control of Serco and Abellio first became involved in the operation of loco-hauled trains in November 2009 following the devastating floods that hit much of Cumbria. With all of the road bridges in Workington damaged or destroyed and the town cut in half, the operator came together with Direct Rail Services, Network Rail and the Department for Transport to offer a free loco-hauled shuttle service to keep local communities connected. Funded by the government, this operated on weekdays between a temporary station at Workington North and Maryport, the trains running between November 27, 2009, and May 28, 2010, by when a new road bridge had been constructed.

Having seen the benefits of loco-haulage to deliver extra capacity, in August 2010 Northern Rail enlisted DRS again to provide four days of shuttle services between Sunderland, Hartlepool and Darlington to cope with the extra demand created by the finishing of the Tall Ships' Races in Hartlepool. A similar arrangement occurred for the visit of the Tour de France cycling event to Yorkshire in July 2014 to deal with the considerable crowds that needed to be moved around the region. Northern hired two-loco hauled sets across two days, one coming from DRS and the other from DB Schenker. The end of the year then brought five Saturdays of Class 47 haulage between Preston and Manchester to provide relief services for Christmas shoppers.

On the Cumbrian coast, January and February 2012 saw DRS undertake a trial loco-hauled service to see if it was viable to provide extra trains for workers at the Sellafield nuclear site in an effort to ease local congestion at peak times. Operated on behalf of parent company, the Nuclear Decommissioning Authority and with the somewhat grudging co-operation of Northern Rail, the services were a success but arguments over who would pay for the operation and take the revenue saw the plan shelved.

Early 2015 brought the surprise news that loco-hauled trains would return on the Cumbrian coast from that May as Northern Rail struggled with a shortage of DMUs. Operating mainly between Carlisle and Barrow, DRS was again charged with providing the locos and stock, this initially taking the form of top and tail Class 37s before a switch to push-pull operation with the use of Mk2f DBSOs. Running until December 2018, by when the franchise was in Arriva's hands, reliability of both the English Electric machines and the driving coaches was patchy, leading to Class 68s providing assistance for a time.

The rail industry earned itself much praise in the aftermath of the Workington floods, the various bodies managing to come together to agree a plan, build a temporary station and get a loco-hauled service up and running within a week of the event. Three days after operations commenced, 37423 *Spirit of the Lakes* bowls along the coast near St Helens on November 30, 2009, with the 2T24 1030 Workington-Maryport shuttle with 47832 *Solway Princess* on the rear. The trains employed some of DRS' own Mk3a FOs along with a Mk2d/e BSO hired from West Coast, in this case InterCity-liveried 9496. The Isle of Man can be seen to the right of the Class 37 and some 30 miles distant. (Dave McAlone)

Northern Rail

By May 2010, normality had more or less returned to Workington with the first replacement road bridge completed and patronage of the shuttles falling rapidly, leading to the services being withdrawn on May 28. Four days earlier, 47712 *Pride of Carlisle* and 57007 were still at work though, top and tailing the 2T40 1850 Workington-Maryport 'Floodex' at Risehow, north of Flimby. (John Eyres)

On the third day of the Sunderland to Darlington shuttles for the conclusion of the Tall Ships' Races at Hartlepool, 57009 leads the way with 47802 *Pride of Cumbria* on the back as they bring the 2Z05 1318 Sunderland to Darlington along the scenic Durham coast at Hawthorn Hive on August 10, 2010. Two loco-hauled sets were deployed for the duration, the other featuring 47712 and 57004 with both employing Cargo-D Mk2s and Mk3s, some of the latter still retaining Wrexham & Shropshire brandings from a previous hire. (Steve Porrett)

LOCO-HAULED - Passenger Trains of the Privatisation Era

Northern Rail

The cold start of 2012 was perhaps not the best time of year to hold the trial for the Sellafield staff trains but nonetheless they were a success, only to be derailed by industry politics. On February 2, 47810 *Peter Bath MBE 1927-2006* crosses the River Mite at Ravenglass with the 5T21 0942 Barrow-Sellafield empty stock working, where it would stable until the late afternoon to form a working to Carlisle. The Mk2 stock was hired from Riviera Trains while Class 37/4s were also employed, the electric train supply being much needed given the condition of Sca Fell in the background. (Dave McAlone)

The coming of the Tour de France to Yorkshire in July 2014 delivered a considerable and lasting boost to the county. For transport operators, it was a major exercise to keep passengers moving between the different stages over the two days. On the Sunday, July 6, this had been made more complex following the failure of 47810 at Blackburn on the Northern-hired DRS set, leading to 57308 *County of Staffordshire* working the 1Z18 1425 Blackburn-Bradford Interchange alone, where it is seen at Walk Mill, Burnley. Fortunately, 20308 and 20309 had been provided in the area in case of problems, the Type 1s dropping onto the other end of the train at Bradford for the remainder of the day. (Neil Harvey)

Northern Rail

The other loco-hauled set hired by Northern for the cycling event was provided by DB Schenker and saw red-liveried 67027 top and tail a Mk3 formation with Royal classmate 67006 *Royal Sovereign*. On July 6, they spent the day perambulating around West Yorkshire, this being the 1L01 0829 Leeds to Hebden Bridge, which is seen at Dryclough Junction, Halifax. Part of Virgin Trains' 'Pretendolino' set made up the passenger stock with DVT 82146 from DB's management train acting as the brake and guard's accommodation. (Neil Harvey)

Following major overcrowding in previous years, Northern Rail opted to run loco-hauled additionals between Preston and Manchester Victoria on the five Saturdays leading up to Christmas 2014. Featuring top and tail DRS Class 47s and Mk2s, the set was out for the entire day shuttling between the two cities, although some legs only ran to and from Chorley or Buckshaw Parkway. On the first Saturday, November 22, Northern Belle-liveried 47790 *Galloway Princess* was provided along with 47818, the former being recorded at Preston having just arrived with the 5Z17 1659 empty stock move from Chorley. (John Eyres)

LOCO-HAULED - Passenger Trains of the Privatisation Era

Northern Rail

With the Cumbrian Coast loco-hauled trains having commenced just over a month earlier, 37409 *Lord Hinton* leads the 2C42 1737 Carlisle to Barrow-in-Furness across Harrington Viaduct on June 23, 2015. At this time, the trains were worked by top and tail Class 37s due to the late arrival of the refurbished Mk2f DBSOs with one of the pair often being a freight-only example, in this case 37606. The absence of the push-pull vehicles also meant BSOs had to be hired from Riviera Trains as cover, both Virgin and Anglia liveried examples being employed. (John Eyres)

The DBSOs were put into traffic from July 2015 after the completion of driver training, modifications to their control equipment having been made to give compatibility with the Class 37/4s via the blue star multiple working system. On April 23, 3016, 37401 *Mary Queen of Scots* propels the 2C40 0842 Carlisle-Barrow into St Bees station. In the background is St Bees School, which was founded in 1583. (Dave McAlone)

Northern Rail

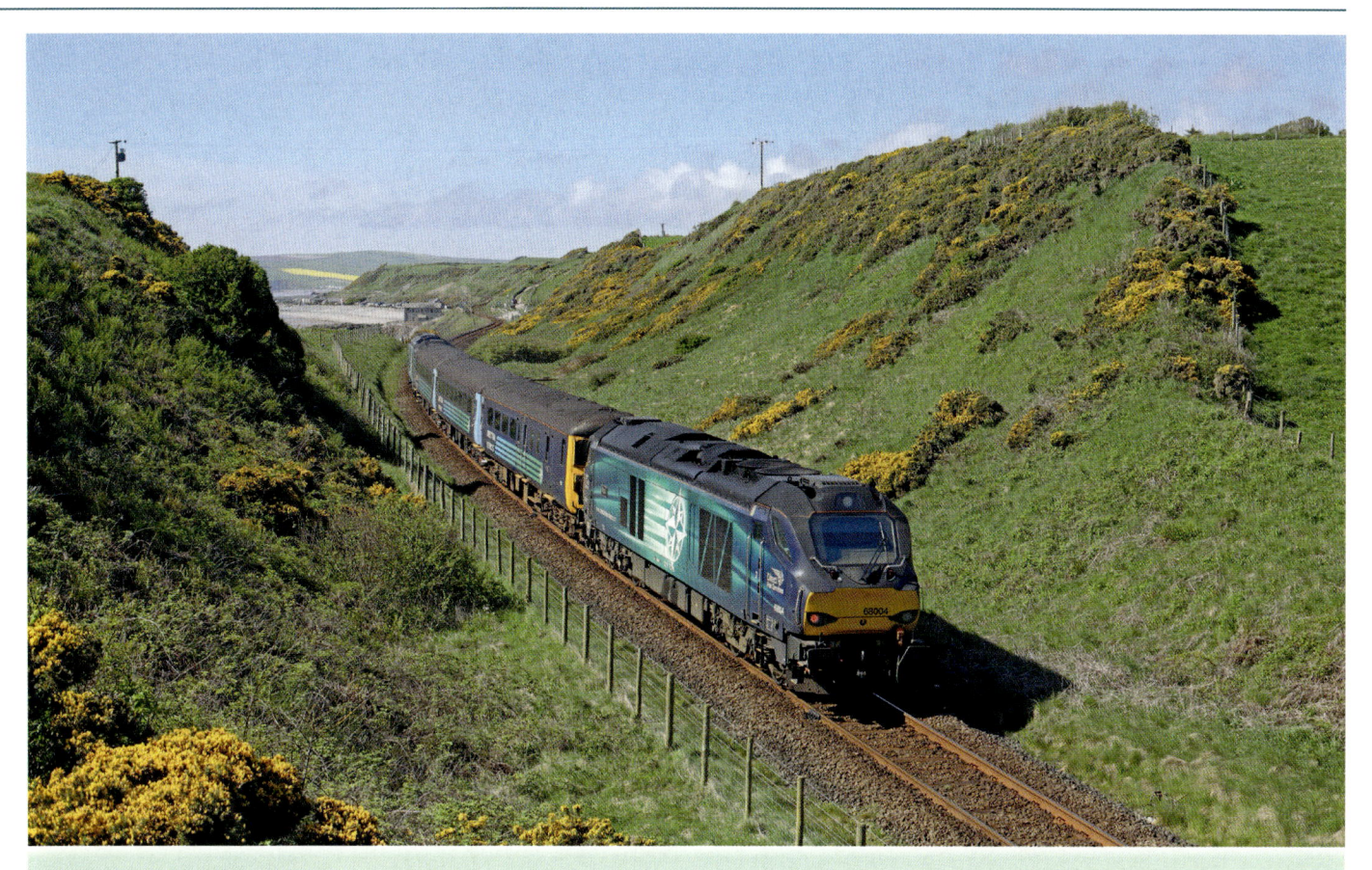

For a time, top and tail Class 68s were drafted onto one set at considerable expense in an effort to improve the reliability of the service after numerous issues with the Class 37s and DBSOs. On May 14, 2018, 68004 *Rapid* brings up the rear of the 2C41 1437 Barrow-Carlisle as 68003 *Astute* powers through the cutting on the single line section at Nethertown. (John Eyres)

Passing beneath the towering cliffs at Parton, 37402 *Stephen Middlemore 23.12.1954-8.6.2013* approaches the village with the 1737 Barrow-Carlisle on May 10, 2017. As with the Anglia workings, the combination of large logo 'Tractors' and the stunning scenery of the Cumbrian coast made it irresistible to photographers. (Dean Cornthwaite)

Welsh Express

Wagging through Wales

Under the remit of its devolved powers, the Welsh Assembly Government introduced a loco-hauled set between Holyhead and Cardiff on December 15, 2008. Intended to improve the rail services between north and south Wales, the train was pitched at business travellers and included first class accommodation along with full kitchen facilities and an on-board chef. Having seen off competition from Grand Union and Wrexham & Shropshire, Arriva Trains Wales was awarded the contract to run the 'Premier Service' or the 'Y Gerallt Gymro' (Gerald of Wales) as it was otherwise known. For many though, it was simply the 'WAG Express' and attracted some negative press for being a costly government vanity project.

The morning service departed Holyhead at 0532 and, running via Crewe, arrival in Cardiff was scheduled for just under four and a half hours later at 0958. The evening return from the Welsh capital was similarly timed with a 1617 departure and arrival into Holyhead at 2049. Motive power initially came from the Class 57/3 'Thunderbird' fleet, where there was now a surplus of locos following the end of loco-hauled services on the West Coast and improved reliability from the 'Pendolinos'.

For the launch of the service, both 57314 and 57315 were repainted in a new two-tone blue Arriva livery as the primary traction while 57313 and 57316 were given a coat of the darker blue only, this being intended as a neutral scheme that could be used by both Arriva and Virgin. As usual though, the needs of the railway won out against such restrictions with the fully-liveried Arriva duo appearing atop Class 390s at times while Virgin sisters occasionally perambulated through Wales. For the first couple of months, two Class 57s were employed on the train, for insurance if nothing else, but this soon dropped to one. The selected coaches received the same two-tone blue scheme with the Mk2f TSOs and BSOs coming from the former Rhymney pool while the Mk3a buffets were former Virgin vehicles.

After three years of uneventful operation, major changes took place during 2012, beginning on March 26 when Class 67s arrived to show the General Motors rebuilds the door. The preceding months had seen 67001-03 receive the same remote fire extinguisher modifications as their Wrexham classmates along with a repaint into Arriva plain blue. Initially, a single loco was deployed with the existing stock but top and tail operation was introduced from that September to allow the train to reverse at Chester, this finally achieving a long-held aspiration of the WAG in routing the service via Wrexham General. The use of two Class 67s was only temporary though and lasted less than a month before switching to push-pull working with a DVT, the changeover having been delayed awaiting refurbished Mk3 coaches.

On the lovely spring evening of May 11, 2009, fully-liveried 57315 departs Hereford with the 1W91 1617 Cardiff Central-Holyhead. For the launch of the service six months earlier, only half a dozen coaches had been prepared and repainted, these being Mk2f TSOs 5965, 5976 and 6183 along with BSOs 9521 and 9539 while there was just one Mk3 buffet, 10249. The latter is seen behind the loco on this occasion with two TSOs and a BSO behind.
(Matthew Clarke)

Welsh Express

Inevitably with no spare buffet car available, when 10249 had to be removed from the set, Arriva was forced to hire 10202 from Cargo-D to maintain the first class and catering arrangements. With its BR blue/grey livery somewhat disrupting the otherwise pleasing look of the train, the evening 1W91 working to Holyhead is seen at Ponthir, to the north of Newport, on July 23, 2009. By the end of the year, the fleet of Arriva coaches had been increased with another buffet, 10259, and a further TSO, 6137. In charge on this day was 57316 in the so-called neutral blue. (Jonathan Lewis)

A second Mk3 push-pull set was introduced from December 15, 2014, this time running between Manchester Piccadilly, Holyhead, and Llandudno. Intended to add capacity to the busy route, Arriva received funding assistance from both the Department for Transport and the by now re-named Welsh Government to launch the service, which required another set of Mk3 coaches but with no buffet or special status this time.

From October 2018, Transport for Wales took over the franchise with both trains continuing to run into 2020, albeit with patchy reliability at times. Like other operators though, the Mk3 stock was not compliant with the new accessibility legislation and was due to come out of service in May. However, the pandemic then intervened and did the job even sooner, both sets being permanently stood down two months earlier.

Prior to normal life grinding to a halt, TfW was well advanced with their replacements, it leasing three shortened sets of Mk4 coaches made redundant from the East Coast Main Line. These had duly received modifications to make them compatible with the Class 67s and staff training was just getting underway when the programme was suspended. Current expectations are that the Mk4s will be introduced to passenger service at some point in the autumn.

With the stock of the 'Premier Service' lying unused at weekends, Arriva Trains Wales was proactive in deploying it to give additional capacity. Such workings were particularly common when a major sporting event was taking place at the Millennium Stadium in Cardiff. On November 6, 2010, 57315 and 57313 are seen top and tailing the 1V77 0808 Holyhead-Cardiff at Bunbury, Cheshire, with the formation strengthened to six Mk2f coaches but with the buffet removed. On this day, Wales entertained Australia in a rugby union match that was lost 16-25. (Phil Chilton)

Welsh Express

On August 9, 2012, 'Gerald' was less than two months away from becoming a push-pull operation with replacement Mk3 coaches. The motive power had already changed that spring with the arrival of the plain blue Class 67s as illustrated by 67003 as it skirts the North Wales coast at Penmaenmawr with the 1W91 1615 Cardiff-Holyhead.
(Terry Eyres)

After years of pressure, the Welsh Government finally got its long-desired routing via Wrexham in September 2012, the need to reverse at Chester having previously made this operationally inconvenient by either requiring a run-round or expensive top and tail operation. Ironically, the latter was required for the first few weeks of the new route due to the late arrival of the Mk3 coaches. On September 19, 67001 and 67002 pause at Shrewsbury with the re-timed 1W94 1821 Cardiff-Holyhead, the shorter journey via Wrexham allowing a later departure for both workings.
(Bushcutta)

104   LOCO-HAULED - Passenger Trains of the Privatisation Era

Welsh Express

The introduction of the Mk3s from the autumn of 2012 gave the 'WAG Express' a fresh appearance with the DVTs looking particularly striking in their Arriva colours. Three of the latter were provided in the form of renumbered 82306-08 while six TSOs were also refurbished, 12176-81 being converted from Mk3b First Opens and re-seated accordingly. The previous buffet cars of 10249 and 10259 were retained with the standard formation being pictured at Newport on August 15, 2016, as 82307 brings up the rear of the 1V91 0533 Holyhead-Cardiff Central with 10259 and three TSOs being hauled away by 67002. (Nathan Williamson)

The morning working from Holyhead is again seen at Newport as 67012 crosses the River Usk while propelling 1V91 towards Cardiff on April 26, 2017. By this time, 67001-03 were no longer the dedicated motive power for the train, indeed at least one of the trio was stood down due to persistent reliability problems. Instead, any of the colourful class could appear as long as they had the necessary modifications, those noted over the years on both the Cardiff and Manchester workings including 67008/10/12-16/18/20/22/23/29. (Mark Few)

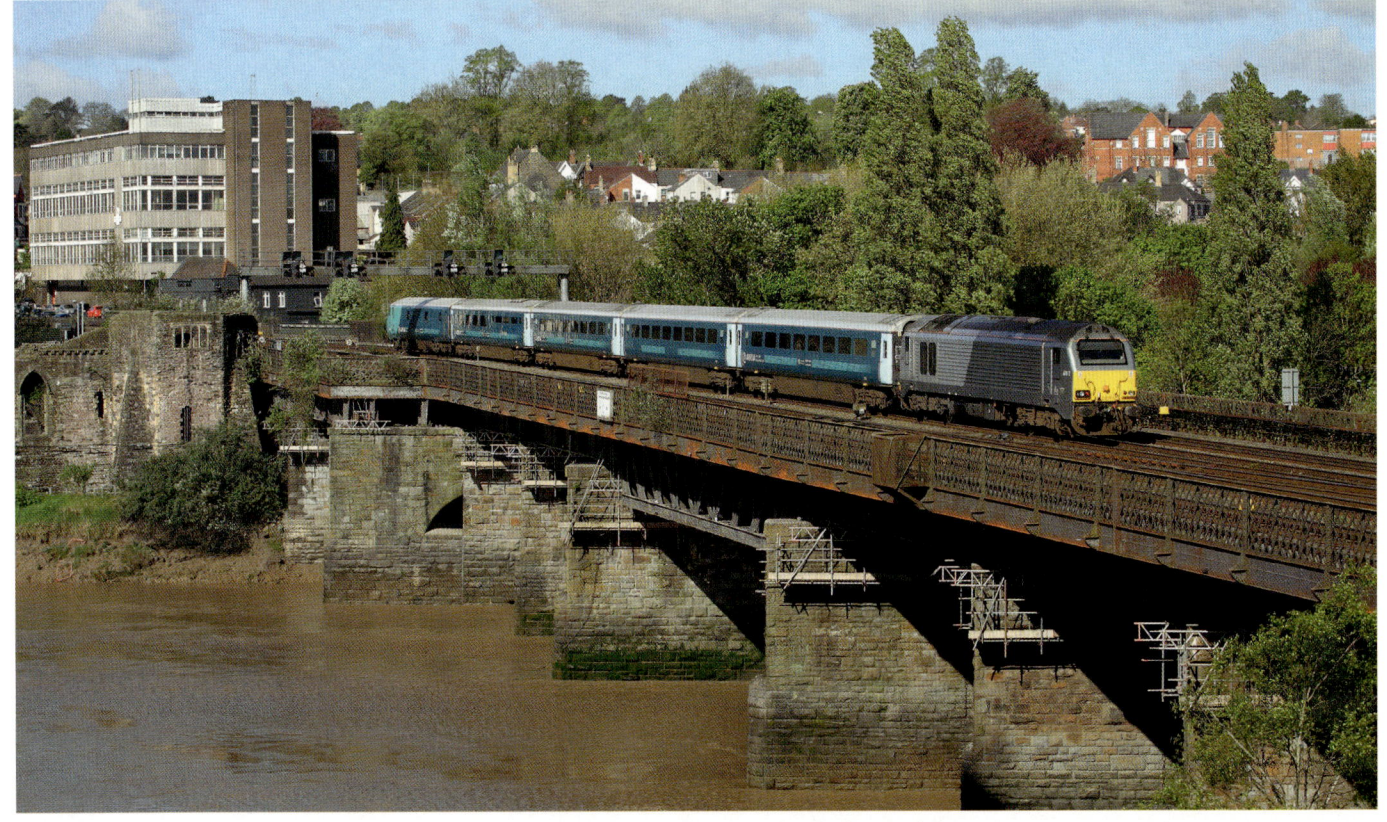

LOCO-HAULED - Passenger Trains of the Privatisation Era

Welsh Express

Less than a month after the second loco-hauled set commenced operation, 67001 passes over Frodsham Viaduct and the River Weaver with the 1D34 0950 Manchester Piccadilly-Holyhead on January 8, 2015. The barge is the *Progress*, which was built in 1965 and saw use on both the Manchester ship canal and River Mersey before withdrawal and sale into private hands in 2012. (John Eyres)

It was the turn of a tired-looking 67022 to take charge of the 1D34 0950 Manchester Piccadilly-Holyhead on May 23, 2018, as it passes through Warrington. This rare view of the West Coast Main Line became possible following vegetation clearance by Network Rail. For the Manchester set, four more FOs were refurbished and turned into standard class vehicles, 12182-84 being Mk3a while 12185 used a Mk3b. No further DVTs were provided though, which left only one spare for the two trains, this occasionally causing an availability problem. (Terry Eyres)

Welsh Express

EWS-liveried 67020 rumbles through the heart of Manchester on April 20, 2017, at it traverses the notorious bottleneck at Oxford Road station on its way out of the city with the 1D31 1650 Manchester Piccadilly-Llandudno. Occupying the rest of the through platforms are two Class 319s and a Class 156. (Simon McComb)

LOCO-HAULED - Passenger Trains of the Privatisation Era

Welsh Express

On October 29, 2019, 67010 was nearing journey's end as it heads across the Isle of Anglesey to Holyhead with the 1D34 working from Manchester Piccadilly. The location is Malltraeth Viaduct, which crosses the River Cefni, near Bodorgan, while the loco's DB red livery is enlivened, or ruined depending on your point of view, by the 'First choice for rail freight in the UK' slogan applied to the bodyside some two years earlier. (John Eyres)

The new order for the Transport for Wales loco-hauled services is seen at Helsby on a training and gauging special on January 30, 2020. With 67025 and the DVT at the other end in TfW colours, the Mk4 formation is a tight fit in the station platform while working the 3Z67 0934 Crewe Carriage Shed-Longsight. With the former East Coast vehicles complying with the accessibility regulations after alterations, these sets should be in service for a number of years, once they do actually get in traffic in a post pandemic world! (David Rapson)

TransPennine

Rebirth for the Pennines

Loco-hauled trains were a daily feature of Trans-Pennine services under British Rail until their demise in January 1991 as the Class 158s were delivered. It was not until July 2014 that its privatised successor returned to the concept, First TransPennine Express following Northern Rail in hiring a loco-hauled set to cope with the demands of the Tour de France coming to Yorkshire.

As part of the subsequent TransPennine Express franchise that commenced in April 2016, a commitment was made to order new train fleets, this including CAF-built Mk5 coaches that would work in push-pull mode with Class 68s leased from DRS. While these began to be delivered from the spring of 2018, numerous problems with the stock along with delays to the driver training programme meant that the first Mk5 set did not enter passenger service until August 2019.

With a higher priority then given by TPE to getting the equally new Class 397 and Class 802 fleets into traffic, 2020 was due to bring a fleetwide deployment for the Class 68 and Mk5s. However, the coronavirus pandemic put paid to these plans with the number of sets in traffic being cut to just two. The second half of 2020 is expected to bring a gradual increase in the use of the trainsets but with full usage still some way off.

For its Tour de France specials in July 2014, First TransPennine Express turned to DRS to supply one complete train, this featuring two Class 47s, five Mk2f TSOs (5971, 6046, 6117/22/73) and Mk2d BFK 17159. On July 5, 47853 and 47841 were employed on two return trips between Liverpool Lime Street and Scarborough with the duo seen approaching Warrington Central on the 1Z87 1322 departure to the east coast. The following day and with 47813 in place of 47841, a more complex Liverpool-York-Leeds-Manchester-Doncaster-Liverpool circuit was covered. (John Eyres)

LOCO-HAULED - Passenger Trains of the Privatisation Era 109

TransPennine

As part of the training programme for the introduction of the Mk5s, TPE leased a number of Mk3 coaches to give its staff experience of working with loco-hauled stock, these mainly coming from the former Virgin Trains 'Pretendolino' set. While plans to use them in regular service were foiled by red tape, a franchise commitment meant that TPE had to run a single loco-hauled train before the end of 2017. This happened on the evening of December 30 when 68003 *Astute* and 68030 top and tailed four of the Mk3s on a single return trip between Manchester Piccadilly and Manchester Airport. In this image 68003 sits on the stops at Piccadilly after the bizarre outing, having brought in the 1Z69 2115 return from the airport. (Tony Woof)

In the second week of Mk5 passenger operation on September 5, 2019, 68027 *Splendid* awaits departure from Scarborough with the 1F62 1041 working to Liverpool Lime Street. The TPE livery certainly provides a striking comparison with the train's more historic surroundings while, in the background, sister 68028 *Lord President* is engaged on driver training duties to York. (Mick Atkin)

On April 24, 2020, 68025 *Superb* lives up to its name as it hauls the 1E31 0954 Liverpool Lime Street-Scarborough across Sankey Viaduct, Earlestown. The picture was taken during a lockdown walk. The pandemic severely curtailed TPE's Class 68 use with only two diagrams left operating during the spring and early summer while other sets were sent into store at various locations. (Terry Eyres)

110 LOCO-HAULED - Passenger Trains of the Privatisation Era

TransPennine

Brutus meets beauty near Kirkham Priory on May 28, 2020, as 68019 powers the 1F72 1534 Scarborough-Liverpool Lime Street alongside the River Derwent. The picturesque spot is a few miles to the southwest of Malton with the railway paralleling the twisting course of the river between the two locations. (Mick Atkin)

Under the lease agreement with DRS, blue-liveried 68033 and 68034 are available for use by TransPennine Express should any of the 68019-32 batch be unavailable. During the spring of 2020, both received the necessary modifications to make them compatible with the Mk5 stock before seeing passenger use to ensure everything was in order. On its first day out with TPE, May 14, 68033 enjoys the evening sun as it powers along between Seamer and Staxton with the 1F78 1834 Scarborough-Manchester Victoria. Its classmate would undertake similar shakedown runs on June 1. (Mick Atkin)

Transport for Wales

A return to Rhymney

When the last loco-hauled workings to Rhymney ceased in 2006, no one would have predicted that 13 years later Class 37s would again be hauling service trains in the Welsh valleys. Yet this was the remarkable situation that occurred from June 2019 as Transport for Wales (TfW) was confronted with a shortage of DMUs. This was in part caused by the late delivery of the Class 769 'Flex' units but, more pertinently, the need to release a large number of units for accessibility modifications ahead of the rule changes on January 1, 2020.

Somewhat reluctantly, TfW was forced to turn to loco-haulage to cover the shortfall with Colas Rail contracted to provide the motive power while Riviera Trains would supply the Mk2e and 2f coaching stock. After an extended period of driver training, passenger services finally began on June 17, 2019, with 37418 working a single morning service from Rhymney to Cardiff Central before an early evening return. These peak-hour workings mirrored the latter years of the Arriva Train Wales operation with the stock stabling overnight at Rhymney and only really doing the bare minimum to justify the hiring costs.

From August 12, a second diagram was introduced after further training was completed, this again being intended for commuters and with 37025 and 37421 operating in top and tail mode. Thereafter, the three 'Tractors' held the fort as reliability allowed with the two Class 37/4s intended as the primary motive power due to their electric train supply equipment, although 37025 did work solo on occasions.

Early in 2020, more DMUs became available to TfW, allowing one diagram to be withdrawn completely towards the end of February while the other was clearly on borrowed time, 37418 working the final train on March 6, 2019. Thereafter, the stock was held in reserve for a while in case it was needed but this proved not to be the case.

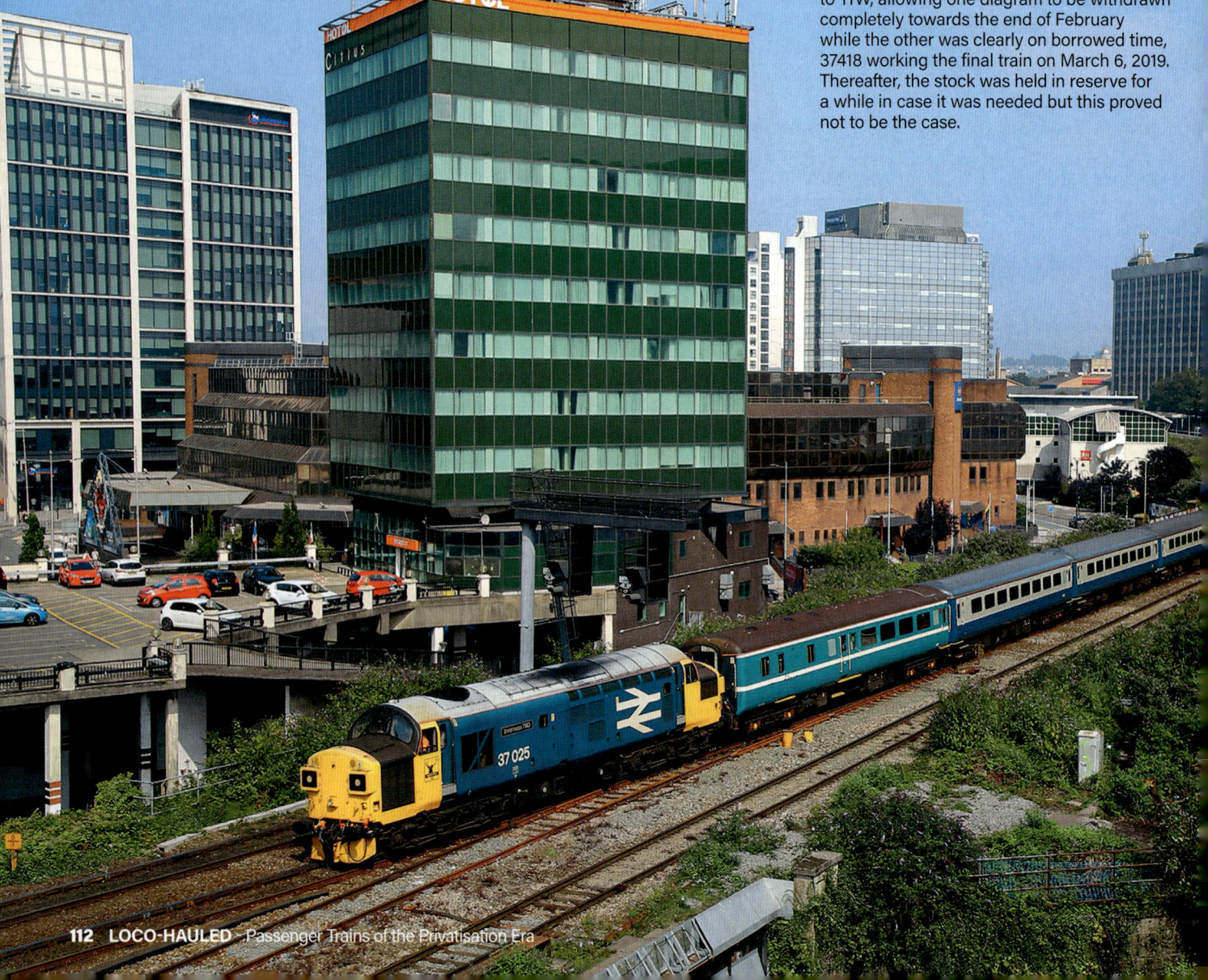

Transport for Wales

Privately-owned 37418 only returned to the main line in February 2019 after an extensive overhaul but it went on to be an integral part of the Rhymney operation on hire to Colas Rail, working both the first and last trains. On June 28, 2019, it is seen approaching Pontlottyn with the 2R20 1701 Cardiff Central-Rhymney with the scenery doing a good job of standing in for its one time haunt of the Kyle of Lochalsh line. Ten Mk2 coaches were employed on the Rhymney services over its duration, the majority being in BR blue/grey (TSOs 5961/98, 6024/54/67, 6158 and BSOs 9507/26) with just TSO 6042 and BSO 9520 finished in Anglia Railways turquoise. (Mark Few)

Having just left Cardiff Queen Street station, 37025 *Inverness TMD* leads the 3Z12 1100 Rhymney-Canton crew training outing through the city centre on August 26, 2019, with 37421 on the rear. The skyline has changed somewhat since the veteran machines were built in 1961 and 1965 respectively and is dominated by the Citrus Hotel and the headquarters of the Admiral Group. Also visible are the Motorpoint Arena, Premier Inn, Cardiff's Ibis Hotel, Brunel House and Cardiff Prison. (Adam Snow)

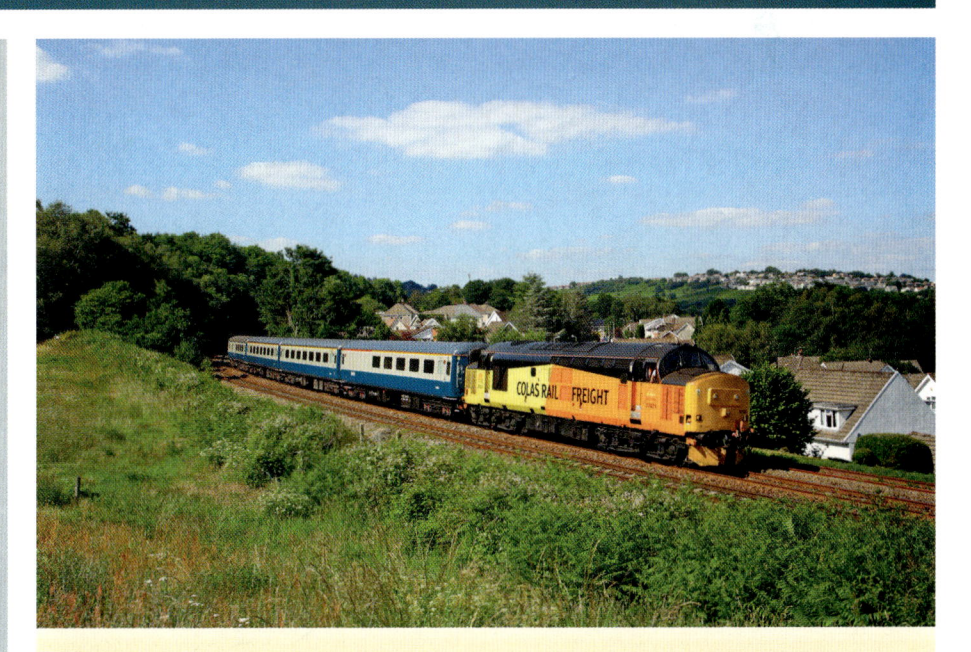

Prior to the introduction of both passenger diagrams, an intensive programme of staff training was required for both drivers and guards as many were unfamiliar with working loco-hauled trains. In particular, drivers only used to DMUs had to adapt their driving techniques to suit the more sensitive Class 37s, which caused problems at times. On a hot July 3, 2019, 37421 rounds the curve at Ystrad Mynach with a 3Z36 1547 Rhymney to Cardiff Canton training run. This rake of Riviera coaches was only used for training purposes as it featured Restaurant First Open (RFO) 1212 along with FOs 3340 and 3386, which were somewhat over specified for commuter use! Completing the set was BSO 9504. (Jamie Squibbs)

Grand Central

Flying from the Fylde

During June 2018, the Office of Rail and Road gave approval for a new open access operation between Blackpool North and Euston. This permission was originally awarded to Great North Western Railway (GNWR) but as the plan developed it was decided to use the established Grand Central brand instead, both being subsidiaries of Arriva.

Five trains a day will run each way between the Fylde coast and London on Mondays to Saturdays with four on Sundays. These will all call at Poulton-le-Fylde and Kirkham & Wesham before making limited stops on the West Coast Main Line at Preston, Nuneaton and Milton Keynes, this slightly odd calling pattern being to avoid issues with Avanti West Coast over revenue abstraction.

From the start, the plan was to use refurbished and shortened Mk4 sets but an initial proposal to utilise Class 91s as the motive power was sadly dropped in favour of Class 90s hired from DB Cargo, denying the one time InterCity flagships a chance to work on the West Coast. The services were originally due to commence running in May 2020 but the pandemic has pushed this date back by 12 months due to the impact on staff training and the drop in passenger numbers.

While some of its Mk4 sets were undergoing refurbishment at Alstom's Transport Technology Centre in Widnes, others were used by Grand Central for both static and main line training. With the coronavirus outbreak putting paid to this, those sets on temporary lease were returned to store while the others were sent to join the overhaul queue. On June 1, 2020, tatty EWS-liveried 90037 *Spirit of Dagenham* was in stark contrast to newly repainted 90026 on the rear as the duo worked the 5Z90 1332 Wembley-Widnes past Slindon with set GC01 for refurbishment, this consisting of Mk4s 12211, 12434, 12310, 10318, 11319 and DVT 82201. (Brad Joyce)

Giving a taste of what 2021 should bring, 90029 leads two sets of refurbished and repainted Mk4s south at Heamies Farm on June 26, 2020, these being GC02 and GC03. The coaches had departed Alstom's refurbishment centre at Widnes that morning and were bound for Wembley depot as 5Z90 to await the resumption of training. Out of sight on the rear was 90026. (Brad Joyce)